# Go-Go Boy

## Memoirs from the Kitchen Floor to the Dance Floor

### DJ Reimer

ISBN: 979-8-9989533-1-6

Library of Congress Control Number: 2025910566

First edition

Printed in U.S.A.

Published by Ingram Spark

*For all those who have loved me unconditionally.*
*Especially you, Mom and Dad*

# CONTENTS

# Author's Note

Writing a memoir like this was never on the bingo card. Then again, neither was go-go dancing, but here we are. At this point in my life, I thought I would be writing policy memos in Washington, D.C., or academic articles in some ivory tower. Instead, I am writing about shaking my ass in noisy nightclubs. Put bluntly, this is not the story I thought I would ever tell, and I don't want my go-go box to turn into a soap box, but my unconventional profession has set the stage for a poignant story about love, community, and the kinds of people you should be dancing for.

I hope to bring you all into not only my experiences but also my psyche. To do that, my inner thoughts will be *italicized* throughout the book. Please note that these internal voices reflect a wide range of emotions and perspectives—sometimes calm, sometimes chaotic, and often contradictory. Occasionally, these thoughts will be presented in the first person, while others are presented in the second person.

In addition, I have a very dark sense of humor and have always coped with stressful situations in my own way. I will describe several challenging experiences that may be unsettling, and my reactions to those experiences may be equally unsettling. Rest assured, I've learned to cope healthily when in times of stress, and the horrendous thoughts that you may read are just that: thoughts.

Finally, while the premise of this book involves my experience as a go-go dancer, I wanted to write a story about not only what happens in the clubs but what happens after the lights come on at the club at the end of the night. My story is not necessarily representative of all go-go dancers; some may have very different experiences from mine. However, I hope that anyone, go-go dancer or not, who has experienced loneliness, chronic unemployment, depression, and despair will feel seen and take solace in the following pages.

Thank you for listening to my story. Showtime.

# PROLOGUE

W*here the hell are my pants?*
　　I screamed internally as I rummaged around in the tiniest dressing room in the world, searching for the pants I had been wearing earlier in the night. The heaping pile of other dancers' clothes all tangled together made my task even more difficult. Sweatshirts, booty shorts, jock straps, thongs, backpacks of varying sizes, and fishnets were strewn about the dressing room, rendering my pants MIA.

It was a frigid and damp night. At just an hour and a half past midnight, I was about to clock out of my very first shift go-go dancing at the Sanctuary, a popular nightclub in West Hollywood. Both my legs and hips were quite sore after shaking and gyrating for about four hours. All I could think about was a steaming hot bowl of clam chowder and crackers that awaited me when I returned home. But this was a fun night, an important night. I found myself filled with mixed emotions, which I promptly put on hold while I searched for the final remaining piece of clothing that remained elusive.

The only other person in the dressing room with me was Jaden, the dance manager and coordinator for dancers at the Sanctuary. I could still hear the beating pulse of the music from the secluded dressing room. The merriment and frivolity would likely continue for another few hours as celebrations raged throughout the busiest, most vibrant piece of real estate in Southern California.

At long last, I managed to discover my neatly folded black jeans on the upper shelf of the dressing room underneath the belongings of the several dozen other dancers. Immediately upon discovering my beloved black pants, I noticed Jaden attempting to keep the dressing room organized.

"Hey, Jaden! I finally found my pants!" I exclaimed proudly.

"Nice! Where were they?" he asked.

"Under a heaping pile of everybody else's crap!" I said.

"Well, welcome to West Hollywood," he shrugged with a grin.

"Now if I can just shake as much glitter off them as possible," I said.

"First rule of WeHo, you will never be rid of glitter, like ever!" he joked.

"Fair point. The other gift that keeps on giving. Do you need any help getting this place tidy before I bounce?" I asked.

"Yeah, sure, if you could just help me move some of these boxes to the corner and toss all the empty water bottles, that would be awesome!" he said.

We proceeded to round up all the plastic crumpled water bottles into the recycling bins. After moving the boxes to the corner and clearing up the tiniest bit of space in the dressing room, I reached out to give Jaden a big, warm embrace. With just one hug, I released so much pressure that had built up over 2023 and was now fully ready to embrace the new year, whatever was to come of it. While still in each other's embrace, I whispered into his ear.

"Thank you so much for everything. Seriously, thank you," I whispered.

"Aw, thank you so much, babe. We loved having you here," he said warmly.

"My pleasure! I had a blast. Please get home safely," I said.

I started to strip out of my uniform, a single pair of black bikini briefs, and held them up in front of Jaden.

"Uh, do we like, recycle these things or something?" I asked awkwardly.

"You are more than welcome to keep it," said Jaden, with a chuckle.

I placed the very damp, skimpy pair of briefs into my gym bag and changed into my real underwear. The feeling of a sweaty under area on fresh, dry underwear was an odd sensation; it was a feeling I would eventually have to get used to. Once fully dressed, I threw my gym bag around my shoulder and gave Jaden one final brief side hug, then headed for the front exit.

West Hollywood's clubs are notorious for being rather crowded, particularly during major celebratory holidays like New Year's Eve. I briskly made my way past the long line for the bathroom, which ended up snaking around most of the club at that point in the night. The haze of humid smoke and multi-colored lights permeated throughout the building. Music pumping the crowd up was set at a volume so loud, I could feel my body hair physically vibrating to the beat. Couples, and sometimes couples with a plus-one, were making out passionately. Some were glued to their phones figuring out which ball drop photo was most worthy of being posted. Others were drunk, crying, and attempting to sing along to the music. Everyone was doing their own thing, lost in their own little world as I wandered by. Suddenly, I was not a dancer anymore; I received no special looks, propositions, or dollar bills. With just a minor wardrobe change, I had gone from DJ the dancer to Whatshisface the patron. I blended in, which at that point in the night and in my life, I was perfectly satisfied with.

As I got closer to the exit, I bumped into my friend, Terry.

"How's it feel, sweet boy?" he said into my ear.

"I'm sorry?" I yelled back, unable to hear what he had said over the blasting music.

"How does it feel, sweet boy?!" he yelled slightly louder.

"I feel great, I'm just ready to go home, have some chowder, and pass out," I said.

"Well, you did great tonight. We're so glad you moved here," he yelled again.

"I'm lucky to have moved," I said.

"Get home safe, handsome. Please text me when you get home," he said.

We shared a longer embrace, and then I meandered past the rest of the patrons before finally making my way out of the bar.

I walked out onto the sidewalk next to a long, narrow street and headed towards my car in the parking garage. Despite having only lived in Los Angeles for a little over a month by that point, I would learn that this type of evening was typical of a busy night in West Hollywood, also known to locals as WeHo. Bright lights reflecting a kaleidoscope of colors painted a landscape accompanied by a cacophony of incredibly loud dance music, shrieking clubgoers, and omnipresent ambulances and law enforcement officials. I did my best to scurry past the groups of messy drunks stumbling in and out of the clubs. Some were jovial and fun, soaking in every minute of the new year. Others were either sober and annoyed, drunk and annoying, or completely passed out on the grassy area of the nearby park.

Strolling merrily through the park to the parking garage, I was filled to the brim with all of the most bittersweet myriads of emotions. Gradually coming down from the emotional high of the night felt rather disorienting as I reflected on the year that had just come to a close. Vignettes of memories flashed in a flurry in my mind's eye. I felt everything. Happiness. Relief. Anger. Hope. Anguish. Laughter. Guilt. Fear. Bliss.

Despite all these complicated and in some cases contradictory emotions, the one prevailing theme I felt very deeply was gratitude. As I continued to process all these feelings at once, I was ultimately grateful for the many lessons I learned in the year 2023.

I unlocked my car door and hopped into the driver's seat, closing the door and finally enjoying the peace and serenity of an empty car. Ringing sounds from four hours in a loud nightclub echoed in both of my ears. I thought that they might assist me in drowning out all that I was feeling, but that was certainly not the case. As cliché as it sounds,

2023 was the most tumultuous year of my life, second to none. It was the most surreal 365 days I had ever experienced, and, with one quick ball drop, it was over. But the good, the bad, and the ugly memories were playing in a loop in my head.

As I sat there weighing my thoughts, I smiled, I grimaced, I laughed, I held back tears, and I felt my blood pressure rise. It was time to go home. After a few deep breaths and performing some exercises prescribed by my therapist, I felt ready to hit the road. My car wound down the long parking garage and made its way to the exit. I paid my parking fare and turned back onto the boulevard to head home.

The car ride home helped calm me down. It had stopped raining, and the traffic was not as horrendous as I thought it would be. The minimal traffic on the road allowed me to soak in my new environment. I was finally becoming familiar with the crossroads and how to navigate myself from A to B. The rainbow-lit orb lights that hang over Santa Monica Boulevard beamed brightly down at the rain-soaked, bumpy road beneath me. It felt like I was sloshing through a vibrant watercolor palette as I made my way back to my apartment. The various colors made me reflect on the diverse range of feelings I was grappling with as I journeyed away from the calamity of the noisy club scene.

I parked my car downstairs in the garage and made my way up the elevator to the top floor. After walking a few steps towards my apartment, I noticed the city landscape from the balcony in the corner of my eye. I decided to take a few extra moments to admire the scenery. Making my way to the edge of the balcony, the myriad of feelings all came back, but this time, the negative feelings were outweighed by those of hope and gratitude.

I gazed at the landscape before me. The Santa Monica mountains were blanketed with homes that resembled a sea of diamonds from afar. The weather was a little chilly but bearable. A brisk wind made its way from below and greeted my face and hair with a welcoming embrace. I closed my eyes again. I felt like I had rewatched the entire previous year and a half on a reel all night long.

Had this all been a dream? Even more so, was I dreaming right now? All of 2023 and the latter half of 2022 felt like the longest period of my life, and yet, there I was on January 1, 2024, living in a comfortable apartment in Los Angeles, and feeling hopeful; cautiously hopeful, but hopeful. It was hard to picture the year ending, let alone ending well. What I was witnessing now with my own eyes was something that would have felt impossible a year ago, even a few months ago. After a few short seconds, I opened my eyes slowly and retired to my room.

# CHAPTER 1

## EASE ON DOWN THE ROAD

I never thought in a million years that I would ever be a go-go dancer. If you had given me a list of a thousand different possible professions, go-go dancing would have most definitely been at the bottom of the list, even three years ago. No doubt, I have always had the performer gene, so the desire to get up on any stage available has long been part of my personality. However, due to my lack of formal dance training and lack of confidence in my appearance, the thought never even entered my mind. Ever.

For most of my life, I have been very underweight and, for a time, had never managed to gain *any* weight. It didn't matter what I did, what I ate, which supplements I consumed, or how often I exercised, I was perpetually stuck at 130 pounds. In the United States, many products can be purchased to *lose* weight, but hardly any products are available to people who want to *gain* weight. I'm unashamed to admit that in high school, after one particular uncomfortable look into the mirror, I went online and tried to see if "Kalteen" bars, a fictional Swedish weight gain bar from the film *Mean Girls*, were sold in the U.S. Not only were they not sold in the country, they were not even a real product.

*Thanks a lot, Tina.*

This view of my appearance lent itself to the idea that I would never be considered good-looking, so I often compensated for my lack of an attractive physique by being the "funny friend." Cracking jokes and being witty were my secret weapons in social settings and in many cases also my defense mechanisms against comments, well-intended or not, about my appearance. This would occur for a greater part of my childhood and well into my post-college years. This would all change in the summer of 2022 when three friends, Jordy, Gavin, and Damien, would each give me a nudge that would ultimately alter my course in the following years.

Jordy and I had known each other for a very long time. We met back in 2007 when I was just a goofy little 12-year-old theater kid performing in a summer showcase. Our school district organized showcases every summer that would include workshops for theater and performance etiquette that would also, on the down low, induce a love of theater for elementary and junior high students. When these students entered high school, the theater department would thus have a wider audition base and theater crew to select from. Jordy, a few years older than me, had just recently graduated from high school, but he stayed in town for the summer and ended up being asked to chore-ograph the summer showcase.

There were a variety of songs from different musicals in this partic-ular showcase/cabaret, but by far the most challenging dance number was "Ease on Down the Road" from the musical *The Wiz*. It is a very high-energy, intense musical number with a fast tempo, and was quite challenging to dance to.

The open secret was that, although there were no auditions for this showcase, the creative director and choreographer knew who the experienced performers were and who would be strategically placed in the back. This was fine because most students did not choose to be in the showcase to be "stars"; indeed, there were no roles like a tradi-tional theatrical production, so there was no desire to be "the best." At the end of the day, everyone just wanted to have fun.

On the other hand, it is always more fun for a performer to be in front than in the back. During our first week of dance rehearsals, we were told to rehearse at home upon learning the choreography: rehearsal is for learning, home is for practicing. The subtle message was that we needed to know the choreography perfectly if we wanted to be placed in the front. Being as competitive as I am, I really wanted to be in the front. After the first day of Jordy's boot camp, it was clear I had my work cut out for me.

The first week was rather intense. I experienced mild but very pesky shin splints and, unlike some of the other attendees who had actually trained to be dancers, had a really hard time grasping the choreography. Simply put, it was blatantly obvious that I was not a dancer. However, I thought with enough enthusiasm and showmanship, I could fake my way up the front row.

After the second week of boot camp, we were told to line up in rows of six dancers per row and had to perform the number in front of Jordy and the director. I wasn't nervous about performing in front of the two of them, I was nervous about not getting the choreography correct. If it had been a vocal audition or a scene reading, I would not have had a single butterfly in my stomach. But this was dancing, not my strong suit at all. I knew that. Time to fake it.

My group's number was called out by Jordy and the director, who were seated a few rows back in the auditorium. The boy-to-girl ratio was always so lopsided at these showcases, so, as I recall, it was me and five girls in a group. We all walked up to the front of the stage as the accompanist repeated the opening vamp from the top of the number. After a few introductory bars, we began to dance.

I noticed that Jordy and the director were spending a lot of time looking at me, but it didn't look like it was for the right reasons. It seemed like they were trying to remain professional and not laugh. After my group's performance, they applauded more heavily than they had for other groups, which I thought meant that I had a shot, but, as I would learn later, they just thought I was being more of a ham. Not only was I not placed in the front row, but I was placed towards the back. So much for faking it.

This trend would continue as I continued to perform throughout high school and beyond. Upon learning the phrase "triple threat" by the end of that summer, I knew almost immediately that my hopes and dreams of performing on stage for a living were implausible. In every musical or production in which I performed, I always dreaded the dance rehearsals. I could carry a tune perfectly fine and didn't have a problem acting, particularly when playing a comedic role. Dancing, however, was always one skill in which I always felt completely out of my depth, no matter what the style of music.

The recognition that my dream to pursue a career as a theater performer would not come to pass was further reinforced by my parents, both pragmatists to the very core of their being. When my father graduated from college, he dreamed of becoming a famous talk show host and disc jockey. I certainly received my sense of humor, desire to perform, and pretty much 99% of my personality from him. After months and even years, his dream of radio stardom would not come to be, so he got a job in non-profit management while my mother taught elementary school. We were comfortably middle class and always lived within our means. I knew that by the time I went to college, I would not be going for a theater degree. The expectation was that I would study something "practical" and participate in performing arts as an extracurricular activity.

While attending university, I discovered a passion and curiosity for foreign languages and other cultures. Noticing China's growing significance on the global stage, I thought that I would be just crazy enough to take a shot at learning Mandarin. I enrolled in an introductory Mandarin course and got straight to work. The simple act of learning how to vocalize the sounds took an entire 10-week-long quarter to learn, not to mention the four different tones.

Additionally, my first Mandarin professor was from Taiwan, an island off the coast of continental Asia that split from mainland China after the Chinese Civil War in 1949. To this day, traditional characters are used officially on the island. Since my professor wanted us to have a solid foundation before switching to simplified, we were required to learn traditional characters first. Chinese is already a massively difficult language to learn, but mastering traditional characters is a whole different mountain to climb.

Many of the traditional characters share similarities with their simplified counterparts, but, as an example, the simplified character 让 has a traditional counterpart that looks like this 讓. Mandarin was always my most challenging subject, but always one in which I felt the most fulfillment. Throughout my time in college, I would write characters down on whiteboards, dinner napkins, and even my car window on a foggy morning for extra practice.

Being the child of highly pragmatic parents, I decided that I wanted to expand my language skills further for professional advancement while having an opportunity to travel the world more. At the insistence of some very resourceful professors, I applied for and received a scholarship to study Mandarin intensively at a university in Taipei, Taiwan, for a full academic year.

I ended up spending two years in Taiwan, which holds a special place in my heart as Taipei Pride was my very first gay pride parade. Since homosexuality is either illegal or, at best, stigmatized in most countries in Asia, Taipei Pride is by far the largest celebration in the entire continent. Handsome boys come to Taipei from countries all around the region: Japan, South Korea, Singapore, Vietnam, etc., to embrace their true selves.

Taiwan also holds a special place in my heart because it was the very first time I ever met a go-go dancer. Nightlife had always been kind of a foreign concept to me. I never really "went out" when I was in college, and going out to clubs and partying was not high on my list of priorities even after I turned 21. My idea of a fun time in college was getting absolutely smashed on boxed wine with my Model United Nations friends and drunkenly ranting about the state of global affairs. While some of my peers were more interested in getting wasted at the club or a fraternity party, my friends and I were busy trying to see how quickly we could say Boutros Boutros Ghali after having way too many glasses of cheap wholesale wine.

In any case, after a couple of months of living in Taiwan, I got to experience my very first pride parade. Taipei hosts their pride event at the end of October during the only three-week period in which the weather is not too hot, humid, or rainy. During my language studies, I lived in a hostel not too far away from my language institute. As fate would have it, a solid majority, if not all, of my male bunkmates at the hostel were also gay. This helped a lot with the culture shock and made Taipei Pride weekend easier to plan.

On the day of the parade, I woke up to the sounds of my bunkmates trying on different outfits, trying to plan the best parade route to follow, and seeing what the appropriate amount of glitter to sprinkle on each of our outfits was. We made our way to Chiang Kai-shek Memorial Hall, named after the infamous military general who escaped the communist revolution and, ironically, was not a fan of the gays.

At the end of the parade route, I noticed a group of very fit Taiwanese men on a float with bubbles protruding in every direction. This particular float, from what I gathered, had already completed its journey on the parade route, and the party had just kept on going. I approached the float and made eye contact with one particularly handsome dancer. His jock strap and matching harness perfectly accentuated his bulging muscles to the point where it looked as though the straps could suddenly snap off without warning. Maintaining eye contact and flashing a flirtatious smile, he gestured for me to get onto the float, which took very little convincing. He said hello to me in English, to which I responded in Mandarin. As was very customary in Taiwan, we both tried to impress each other with our language abilities before taking a selfie together. My hormones and adrenaline ran high, and I grabbed the center of his harness and pulled his muscular chest closer to me for the photo.

After we snapped a few sexy photos together, the float began to move, and the handsome dancer indicated that I needed to step back down to the street. We shared a brief kiss, and I hopped off, waving goodbye to him. Stupidly, we did not exchange social media profiles, so that was the last I saw of him.

As the float moved up the street, I paused to watch the dancers. This form of performing was very foreign to me. I knew there were male strippers who strip down to next to nothing and entertain big crowds in Las Vegas or somewhere like that. I had seen Magic Mike over a hundred times and loved watching that group of actors dance around on a stage in next to nothing in front of a highly stimulated crowd.

But this was different. The style and substance of this kind of performance were very unique. They weren't commanding the full stage like the strippers I had seen clips of in the past. They were all wearing identical jock straps with matching harnesses and were dancing in one place. Unlike musical theater, they were confined to a limited space and had to dance in a somewhat provocative manner. I had never seen anything like it before. It intrigued me, but, given my understanding of my appearance and lack of dance skills, I assumed that this was another dream that would not come to pass.

When my scholarship concluded, I decided to remain in Taiwan to teach English. This gave me the opportunity to travel all around the world. I spent time traveling in many parts of East and Southeast Asia as well as Australia. During the winter of 2018, I was even able to attend the Winter Olympics in South Korea with a childhood friend of mine who had been living there. After Asia, I spent a few months in Mexico in an attempt to obtain proficiency in my third language, Spanish.

The excitement and joy from wanderlust that I felt throughout those years screeched to a halt when the entire world shut down in March 2020. It felt almost like I was having the best time at the hottest club, and then all of a sudden, the lights turned on, the music turned off, and I had to go home. My pragmatic parents encouraged me again to broaden my professional career opportunities, so I enrolled in a master's program in San Diego.

Similar to my experience in Taiwan, I spent hours in the library reading complex academic articles, writing academic papers of my own, and grading undergraduate papers as a teacher's assistant. On some of the very rare occasions when I was able to go out, other grad students and I loved to visit the famous Hillcrest district in San Diego. We would drink and cut a rug on the dance floor, pretending that we didn't have a million and one things to do when we returned to school.

One particular night, we went to a bar that had a lot of go-go dancers. The club was crowded on a Friday night, the music was unbearably loud, and several elevated boxes were occupied by very muscular, sweaty men in very tight briefs shaking their hips in every direction. They looked similar to the go-go dancers I had seen when I lived in Taiwan. I was starting to make progress at the gym when I hired a personal trainer in grad school, but two months of progress were not sufficient for my self-esteem. These guys were extremely muscular and toned, and it reaffirmed the assumption I had that this would be a stage I would never occupy.

After I graduated in June 2022, I spent some time backpacking through Europe and the Mediterranean Sea. Since I was becoming steadily more confident in posting photos of myself, I ended up taking a lot of photos by the picturesque beaches. Some photos where I was wearing a skimpy Speedo, or less, felt more appropriate for posting for a limited audience. Certain social media platforms allow users to post content for a select number of followers. I set up this secret group for followers that I knew would appreciate seeing more skin than my family and friends would.

One photo I posted in particular set off this course of events. The final country on my itinerary, Greece, was definitely my favorite. The highlight of that country was Santorini, the small southern island with the famous Oia village full of white homes facing the most breathtaking blue water in the entire Mediterranean Sea. I went on a boat tour that took our group around the entire island. Around lunchtime, we were brought to a very remote part of the island where the entire economy is essentially restaurants for tourists. There were restaurants on both the sea level and higher up in the hills, but the latter required a bit of a trek on foot. Most tourists in our group decided to patronize the sea-level restaurants, both because they had a beautiful view of the water and also because the trek up was extremely windy and steep on cobblestone roads that felt ancient. Since I was in an adventurous mood, I decided to make the journey to the restaurants on top of the hill.

Greece happens to be the setting for the classic ABBA-based

musical *Mamma Mia!*, so, as a theater gay, I seized upon the opportunity to embrace "the culture" by blasting the soundtrack on my trek up the hill. It was a very long, winding road that felt very steep, but I knew would lead me to a better, picturesque view of the island. About halfway through, I noticed that not a single person from my tour had followed me. In fact, not a single person from any boat tour was interested in hiking up the hill. After looking around both corners of this zigzagging hill, it was very clear that I was completely alone. Picture time.

The view from the trail was stunning. The water in Greece truly does seem far more exquisite and bluer than the rest of Europe. You could easily see the other scattering of mini islands that surrounded Santorini and the clusters of massive boats that carry tourists from site to site. The background was set. Since I didn't have a tripod or a photographer at my disposal, I had to be creative with a stand for my phone. Miraculously, my phone stayed erect while wedged in between some of the rocks, and all I had to do was pose. Typically, I like doing multiple poses for a single video and then going back and screenshotting the poses I like the best.

I looked to the left, I looked to the right; the coast was clear. First, the shirt came off; it was hot as hell anyway, so this wasn't required to be sneaky. The sprayed suntan lotion would not only protect my skin from the sun but would also provide a glossy, shiny appearance that would enhance the photo without a filter. Next came the gym shorts. I was wearing a Speedo underneath for the diving part of the tour that would happen after lunch. Alright, down to just a Speedo and my shoes, one final check around the corners, and it was time for naked DJ.

The feeling of being naked is so liberating, particularly on days with weather as stunning as that day had. Nothing beats natural sunshine and vitamin D hitting every inch of your bare skin. I walked to the edge of the road and I turned around. I posed here, I posed there. It was important to get as many options to choose from as possible later. It is astounding how my phone managed to stay upright for so long, but thankfully, I got a long enough video to be able to screenshot plenty of options.

The rest of the day I spent admiring the beauty and warmth of Santorini, capped off with watching the sunset from the villages of Oia. This was by far the most beautiful location I had visited on the trip, possibly ever. I loved basking in the serenity of warm sunshine cascading down on choppy blue waves while little white and blue homes stood watch over the towering cliffs.

The next day, I woke up and stood impatiently at the dock waiting for the ferry to whisk me off to Athens. As conspicuously as I could, I slowly scrolled through the footage and tried to take some screenshots. Wow. I actually didn't hate what I saw.

*See? This is why you hired a trainer! It paid off! Ok, but you're not a 10. You're like a solid 6, maybe a soft 7. But only in this lighting and angles. Whatever, the best is yet to come. You can only go up from here.*

I settled on one particular pose that was classy enough to be considered a tasteful nude but also sexy and fun enough to look like I was enjoying myself. After I selected a filter, I added music from *Mamma Mia!*, of course, and uploaded the photo to the group of my close friends.

I charged my phone and waited for my ferry to arrive. It was delayed, so I decided to browse my social media feed for a bit. Lots of supportive messages from friends, happy that I was "living my best life" and, since this was a thirst trap, I also received plenty of salacious replies.

One of them was from Jordy, the showcase choreographer that I had not seen or heard from in about ten years.

"Damn girl, you grew up!" he commented on the photo.

It was nice to receive a compliment like that, especially from someone who, for a long time, had always viewed me as a dorky little goober.

After an incredible summer, the magical trip to Europe concluded, and I came home with a full passport, a smartphone full of photos, and a head full of dreams. In retrospect, most of these dreams were not realistic. I had assumed that after over ten years of studying my ass off, graduating undergrad with high honors, living abroad to study Mandarin and Spanish, obtaining a graduate degree, and just being an overall goddamn delight that I would instantly find a job.

How unbelievably wrong I was.

The trip to Europe ended with me returning home to live with my parents in Visalia for what I had hoped would be a temporary amount of time. July went by, August went by, and September went by. Time kept passing, and I felt like my credentials were not landing me the kind of post-graduate life that I had planned. I applied for multiple jobs a day and would only hear back weeks later, if at all. Of the thousands of jobs I applied for, only about 2% would offer me an initial interview. Despite what felt like constant failures in the professional realm, I did not stop going to the gym.

It was around this time that I could feel myself starting to get depressed. Had I not paid so much for a personal trainer in graduate school, I likely would have stopped going to the gym at that point. Nevertheless, I persisted. It was all I had to do, so I was able to increase my regimen. First from 45 minutes to an hour, then to an hour and a half.

I needed something else to occupy my time and get me out of the house, so I volunteered to work on a campaign for a congressional seat close to my hometown. This would require a lot of walking, so additional exercise didn't hurt.

While we did not win the election, I was introduced to my best friend Enrique, who was tasked with organizing the volunteers. Another Valley local, Enrique, also had a high level of interest in politics and public policy. We clicked almost instantly and, although we came from different sides of the left spectrum, could talk for hours on end about both domestic and international politics. He had, and still has, a very infectious laugh and a cheery disposition at all times. To this day, I don't even think I have ever seen him whine or complain about anything.

By the time the election ended in November, I had assumed that my days being unemployed were numbered. Even though our candidate lost, I thought the connections I made and cultivated during the campaign at volunteer functions, activist workshops, and campaign events would have landed me *some* kind of job. Despite a few promising interviews, I remained jobless.

I felt the spiral beginning to worsen with each passing rejection email. Negative thoughts crowded my mind and began to affect my self-esteem, so I began drinking more to drown the thoughts out. At first, it was just a few drinks before I fell asleep. Then I started drinking more frequently and without a chaser.

Often when I felt the urge to drink, I called my friends Damien and Gavin, a couple in Visalia I had met the previous year. Both of them were a few years older than I, but they were the kind of guys I could always count on to rant to about my problems or just enjoy a pleasant evening. This became a routine, particularly when I was unemployed: I would go over to Gavin's house, he would already have something frying in the kitchen, and Damien would be situated on a table on the backyard patio puffing a cigarette with my drink already prepared on the table across from him.

I went over to Gavin's house a few days after the election. This one particular gathering felt a little less pleasant than before; our gatherings were always so jovial and fun, filled with laughter and sometimes drunken lip-syncing to music on Gavin's vinyl record player. Empaths that they were, they could always tell within an instant that I was not in a good mood. After the series of losses and rejection letters, they could sense the palpable frustration in my demeanor.

"Everything is going to shit," I responded to their question regarding how things in my life were going.

"Yeah, we've kind of noticed. You're not exactly known for your subtlety," Gavin said as he poured me his signature drink, vodka mixed with synthetic grape-flavored soda.

"Yeah, I'm going to need you to put a little more happy juice in there for me, guapo," I said as Gavin started recapping the vodka bottle.

Due to the cold November weather, we were situated inside. Gavin's living room is very large, welcoming, and truly the perfect place for hosting. We sat in our usual positions, Damien and I on the couch and Gavin in his armchair on the opposite side, facing the couch. I began to rant about feeling lost and beginning to feel jaded and cynical about my career prospects and life in general. Both listened attentively, with Gavin occasionally refilling my vodka soda.

"I don't know what I'm going to do. The campaign seemed promising, and even after we lost, a lot of the people I worked with were telling me they would help me get a job. One volunteer I worked with even gave me an hour-long pep talk on this one particular job working for a congressman and how I'd be a shoo-in if I hit the right notes and said the right thing during the interview. Well, I applied, and they still have not returned my calls or emails. Even after this nice lady called the office three times on my behalf, they didn't respond," I said. "I should just barge in somewhere and start working Erin Brockovich style."

They both laughed; even when I'm at my saddest, I can't seem to tame the little court jester inside of me.

"You would think that with your language skills and your educational background that you would have an easy time getting a job," Gavin said.

"You would think," I said as I took a big swig of the drink.

"Have you tried bartending or being a waiter somewhere?" Gavin asked.

"Well, define try. Because I have *tried* applying to lots of places, and they never get back to me. I don't know if there's like a firewall or something I can't get past but all I know is that I click the buttons to apply online somewhere and then I sit on my ass everyday day waiting," I grumbled.

"What about retail or fast food?" Gavin suggested.

"All due respect to the people that flip burgers and scan merchandise, but I did not spend the last nine years of my life studying my ass off to work retail or fast food. It's essential work, but I don't want to get stuck in a low-wage job in this town and not advance my career," I said.

"Well, what about your friend Enrique? Can he help you get a job?" Gavin asked.

"He's been trying, but he didn't have much seniority in the campaign, so his recommendation is solid but will only go so far. He's very sweet and kind, but this business isn't," I said with a hint of annoyance.

Gavin took my point, then proceeded to take my empty glass. He disappeared into the kitchen, and that's when Damien started staring at me with this look.

I need to explain this look. Damien's handsome, masculine facial expressions would from time to time give me this look. It was a look filled with affection, pride, and encouragement. It was a sort of look that said, "I know that you're going places, kid." Every time I would be passionate about a subject or telling a fun story, he would just look over at me, beaming. It made me feel wanted, cared for, and seen.

"The fuck are *you* looking at?" I sarcastically scowled.

Damien's disposition didn't change a bit.

"Have you ever thought about go-go dancing?" he asked, maintaining that look.

I jokingly looked behind me as if he were talking to someone else.

"I'm sorry, sir, are you talking to *me*?" I responded.

"You know, Flash and Vertigo in Fresno have dancers from time to time. I have no idea how much they would pay you, but it's worth looking into," Damien said.

I stared back at him with *my* look which is a "are you out of your mind" kind of face. I immediately burst into laughter. That's when Gavin rejoined the conversation.

"What is so funny, you two?" Gavin asked coming into the room.

"Well, it seems that your boyfriend is drunker than I am right now and he's pitching some goofy ideas about what I should do for work," I said.

But Damien didn't flinch.

"I am being completely serious, DJ," Damien said.

"Serious about what?" Gavin asked.

"I told him he should try to find a way to go-go dance at either Flash or Vertigo Bar," Damien said.

"Isn't that crazy?" I said, continuing to laugh.

"Um, I mean it's a different kind of job, but yeah, I could see it," Gavin said.

"Ok, how about now I give *you* guys some career advice, y'all should go into stand-up comedy or something because that's hilarious," I said.

"DJ, listen. You are charming and charismatic, and we've both noticed the progress you've been making on your body. You may not see what we're seeing, but trust me. You have what it takes," Damien said sincerely.

I paused. Even when I'm tipsy, it's easy to read a room, and I could finally tell that he wasn't joking, nor was Gavin. But this was very bizarre; given my history with dancing as an activity, it was surprising that someone was suggesting that I should not only dance in public but that I would be good enough to be able to make money from it. I began to feel a dissonance that I have felt many times since then: a gap between what I hear people saying in my ears and what I am physically seeing with my own eyes.

I didn't believe them when they said I ought to give it a whirl, but it did pique my interest. I imagined what it would be like to be dancing in a club and people putting dollar bills into the waistband of my underwear. Performing was one of my great joys, but I never thought it was even remotely something that I would be able to do. Even so, I shrugged off the possibility; it still just didn't seem like something I should even think about doing. My confidence in my body was certainly not zero anymore, and being out of work for several months afforded me a lot more time to go to the gym and focus on my physique. Nevertheless, my initial gut reaction was telling me that this was not going to happen.

A week later, I received a phone call. It was from Jordy.

# CHAPTER 2

## FRIGID BITCH

Before this phone call, my contact with Jordy since that summer showcase had been extremely minimal. We exchanged friendly birthday messages on each other's social media profiles and maybe an occasional comment on a post, but never regular back-and-forth over a phone call or even a text. We performed in the musical *Grease* together one summer, but did not have very many scenes together. Apart from my saucy photos from my European sojourn a few months prior, I had not heard much from Jordy until he called me that night.

"Jordy?" I asked.

"Hey, it's me, bitch," Jordy said.

Jordy liked to be dramatic, even in a greeting.

"How's it going, boo? I haven't seen you in a minute!" I said.

"Well, I'm good. Still at the salon, getting all the tea from middle-aged ladies and all the drama. You know how it is," Jordy said.

*I actually do not know how it is. I don't have a job.*

"That's great to hear!" I said.

"Yes, yes. Well, I don't want to keep you for too long, but I had a question I wanted to ask you," he said.

I hate this question so very much. I don't care if you're my mother, cousin, lover, ex-lover, acquaintance, friend, or a random stranger from the street. That question bothers me to no end. Just ask the damn question, you don't need to preface it with anything!

"Sure, what's up?" I responded calmly.

"Well, have you ever been to Flash?" he asked.

"I have not. I know people who are frequent fliers to that club, but I have not personally been in it myself," I said.

"Ok, well, this coming Saturday, we have our monthly bear event, and we are a few dancers short," he said.

*Dancers? Did he just say dancers? Like, go-go dancers? He can't possibly be asking me to dance at this event, can he? Well, what else is he asking me to do? Work security?*

"Are you interested?" Jordy asked intently.

I paused. This random offer to go-go dance came as a complete shock to me. To recap: Jordy, the choreographer I had performed with as a youngster, a youngster who *could not dance for shit*, was asking if I would perform as a go-go dancer. And at a *bear* event? I'm not thickly built and don't have hair all over my body. I thought he was out of his mind.

"Well, I'm flattered that you asked me," I responded.

"But?" Jordy inquired.

Honestly, the real hesitation was that I knew very well what my abilities were, and they were not at all related to dancing. I trained to be a diplomat for heaven's sake. How much money could I possibly earn in one night that would be worth the risk of having a photo of me in a thong or jockstrap popping up online and eventually making its way to an oversight committee? I was desperate for the cash, sure, but I was uncomfortable with taking the risk.

"I mean, it's a bear night, right? Aren't there other beefier, hairier guys out there that would be better suited for an event like that?" I asked.

"Oh, honey, you will be fabulous. Trust me, you know the valley crowd won't judge. Also, everyone will be drunk, so I think you'll be fine," he assured me.

*He remembers how I danced, right? Or rather, how I tried to dance. Does he not remember I was in the second-to-last row, specifically due to my inability to dance? That's ok; just keep a level head.*

I paused again, and my brain started to buffer. This would be the first actual money that I would be able to make since I was a teacher's assistant the previous June. I was in no position at all to say no to an opportunity.

On the other hand, the likelihood of being photographed, even by a well-meaning friend, could threaten all that I had worked incredibly tirelessly for since I turned 18. Ten years of reading countless newspaper articles, burying my face into mountains of books on foreign policy, becoming proficient in two foreign languages, and spending time away from friends and family abroad could all have been in vain because of one bad photo op.

"Are you still there?" Jordy asked.

"Yeah, give me a second," I responded.

My eyes closed, and I took a long, deep breath. Memories started to illuminate my mind non-chronologically. Myself dancing at the summer showcase and being put in the back row. The sizzling summer sun baking my naked skin in Greece. Looking into the mirror in high school and wishing I weren't so skinny. Creating a makeshift gym at home during the pandemic of 2020 so that I could get ahead. Drinking heavily the previous week as I sought to drown out the feelings of self-doubt. And then came 'the look.' I remembered how Damien looked at me when he and Gavin brought up the idea of go-go dancing, placing it even in the realm of possibilities. And now my moment was here: I was being asked to perform, for money, for real. I pictured Damien giving me that smirky, proud look he had given me in Gavin's living room.

"Fuck you, Damien," I muttered under my breath, rolling my eyes.

"What was that?" Jordy asked.

"I said, fuck yeah, Jordy. I'm in," I said.

"Yes! Oh my god, I'm so excited to be on stage with you again, queen!" Jordy exclaimed so loudly that I pulled my phone a few inches away from my eardrum. "Ok, so the theme is Playboy. So, make sure you have a few fits that go with that. Hope you haven't skipped out on cardio. Bob, the promoter, is going to be hosting us at his house beforehand so we can get ready. I'll text you the address. It's the Saturday after Thanksgiving, so it'll be pretty packed."

I felt conflicted: lots of people meant more tips, but lots of people also meant more phones snapping pictures, more eyeballs, more witnesses. Whatever. I knew where my priorities were: time to make that money.

After providing me with all the details of what the night would entail, I hung up the phone and felt the deepest sense of whiplash I had ever felt.

*What in the world just happened? More importantly, why now? Was this a coincidence or something? Gavin and Damien nudged me to dance, and then all of a sudden, someone who I hadn't seen in years was hitting me up to ask me to go-go dance? Is this a sign?*

Fate or coincidence, I had already made my decision. I was going to dance.

The first order of business was ordering an outfit. It needed to be revealing, but I was still hesitant to wear a thong or jockstrap in public. I went online and started browsing. Symbolically, a summary of my previous purchases and searches popped up. It was all books about foreign policy, Asian history, and politics. After this online shopping session, my search history would look quite different than before.

Creating the look was critical. It was about staying on theme, of course, but I wanted to make sure I could look as sexy as possible without revealing too much skin. This was a formidable task, but I was trying to balance the two as best I could. It was almost as if I was trying to balance my two separate identities: my already-cultivated professional, diplomatic side with my newly-developing, shall we say, sexy side.

With the balance in mind, I purchased a pair of very tight-fitting leather trunks. They were scandalous enough to look the part but covered enough of the goods. There were tons of bunny ear options online with varying reviews; I always take online reviews with a grain of salt, but these reviews were truly all over the place. I'm not sure why costume bunny ears on the internet are so controversial, but the reviews indicated that this was the case. The algorithm must have caught on that I was buying something Playboy-related because I immediately received recommendations for a silky red bathrobe, a pair of aviator sunglasses, and a wooden pipe. For fun, I purchased all three of them. After buying some costume ears, cuffs, and a bow tie, I sat at my computer for a few minutes, just staring.

The adrenaline began to wear off after a few minutes. Everything was happening at the speed of sound. My coping mechanism, humor, was instantly activated. I chuckled at the fact that my suggested purchases online went from books by Madeline Albright and Frances Fukuyama to jock straps, combat boots, leather straps, and harnesses. Since internet algorithms tend to know more about you than you do, part of me felt like this was a sign of things to come.

*This is just going to be a one-time thing. There's no way that I can possibly make a career out of this, right? It'll just be a fun night that will nab me a few dollars, and then I'll be able to use it as a funny story sometime in the future. Maybe when I'm a diplomat a few years down the road, I'll tell the story of the one time I go-go danced when I'm at a cocktail party or something. Idiot, you're ruining all your future job prospects. This isn't even something you were meant to do. You're going to look ridiculous. None of those outfits are flattering on you; just give up. Give up now.*

My disbelief did not dissipate when I received my outfits in the mail a few days later. I grabbed the plastic packages and immediately dashed for the bathroom, as though I had stolen a Playboy magazine. Ironically, it was *me* who would now be the Playboy.

After safely arriving in the bathroom, I unwrapped my purchases as quickly as I possibly could and threw them onto the counter. Not stopping even for a second, I threw on the tight leather shorts and bathrobe. Next came the sunglasses and the wooden pipe.

*Is this what I'm supposed to look like? Come on. You're trying to show off the goods, why the hell are you hiding behind a goddamn bathrobe. You look ridiculous, you're too young to be in that bathrobe. Be a slut instead!*

I removed the sunglasses, removed the robe, and stared at myself in the mirror for a few minutes. Not knowing how I should feel, I removed everything and stared at myself in the mirror. A completely blank slate; I felt almost like an avatar at the beginning of a video game.

*You could be anything in the next few years, but this is where you are now. Embrace it.*

Two years earlier, I was barely comfortable enough taking my shirt off in the pool and thought my days of performing on a stage were long gone. Now, I would be performing on a platform in close to nothing.

To inspire more confidence in myself, I suited back up in each of my different bunny outfits and quickly snapped a few photos on my phone. I scrolled through the photos and didn't hate what I saw. The gym progress I had made over the past year was apparent, but I continued to let the stupid voices in my head tell me otherwise. I put my phone away and went to my room.

The night before, I told my parents that I would be "going out." They were, and still are, very supportive allies, but this was a whole new world to them. There were several prepared speeches I made about what I was doing and why I was doing it, but I decided to scrap them. I thought to myself, if *I'm* having a hard time grasping this, it'd be best to keep things vague, at least for the time being.


As fate would have it, a group of my straight friends happened to be hosting a Friendsgiving meal late in the afternoon on the day I was set to perform. This was a group of my theater friends from my childhood, so they weren't necessarily shocked by the idea of me performing live, but they did have a few questions about my pants, or lack thereof.

Explaining certain elements about gay culture to straight people has always amused me; even though we are all technically communicating in the same language, it feels as though I am back in my days living abroad, where I constantly had to find the right words to explain myself in another language. There have been countless times when even allies have a hard time grasping certain facets of gay culture; go-go dancing is certainly one of these things.

I arrived at Friendsgiving about 15 minutes early. The hostess, my best friend Lauren, greeted me with a warm hug at the door while her husband, Brad, held back their sweet dog, Rex. Once I was in the house and had removed my shoes, Brad released their hyper-friendly hound, and I embraced him. I hugged the aforementioned doggo as he was overcome with joy and spun around in circles filled with excitement. I've always thought that Rex is the dog version of me.

"You're a little overdressed, aren't you?" Brad sarcastically quipped.

"You're so funny. Have you burned the turkey yet, or have we learned from last year?" I retorted.

Brad and I always tried to see who could out-quip the other with insults. Both of us grew up as the youngest in a household of only boys, so we often emulated brotherly behavior towards one another. His wife, Lauren, and her sister, Michelle, grew up with only sisters, so they were like the big sisters I never had, and I was like the little brother that they never had.

Friends began to file in one by one, and eventually, we had a full room of hungry friends ready to dig in and enjoy company. I had announced on my social media feed that I would be go-go dancing that night in Fresno. Many attendees that day greeted me with a hello and a bit of a wink and nod that night. A few also echoed Brad's quip about me wearing too many clothes, to which I responded with the same canned response.

The meal was delicious and satisfying. Friendsgiving has become one of my favorite holidays, particularly with this crowd of thespians. The joy I've found in theater and performing is that it brings together people who, under any other circumstance, would perhaps not socialize together. It was a beautiful evening catching up with friends old and new, but toward the end of dinner, I was ready to ditch the cute little sentimental vibe and talk to my gal pals about my impending evening of debauchery.

Some of the parents brought their kids over to the couch to play with the other house pets, which gave the rest of us a chance to discuss the night out of earshot.

"Are you nervous?" asked Serena, who, next to me, is probably the wildest out of the bunch.

"I honestly don't know what to think yet," I said. "I'm kind of just going along with it."

"Did you have to buy what you're going to wear, or are they going to give you a uniform or something?" asked Lauren.

"Well, I may or may not have snapped a few photos already in my outfit—"

Before I could even finish the sentence, the girls asked me to share the pictures I had taken in the bathroom.

This was always an amusing exercise: witnessing straight people reacting to things that, to a gay person, were not particularly noteworthy. This group of predominantly straight, somewhat tipsy women squealing and giggling at my photos in my uniform perplexed me.

*Am I about to make a huge mistake? No, they're giggling because they're not used to seeing you with so few clothes. Chill, you'll be fine. No, they're laughing like the crowd will be laughing at you tonight. Get used to this, buttercup.*

The theater community I grew up with was always extremely welcoming and positive. This group was never short on compliments. Besides, I was not only one of the youngest of the group, but I was also never seen as "hot" by my friends. On top of everything, of course, the bunny costume did look rather cliché.

"I can't believe one of our friends is a stripper! And it's one of our *guy* friends!" Serena cackled as she took another sip of spiked cider.

"Well, what we do is not technically stripping," I corrected.

"I mean, that *is* a lot of skin you're showing," Lauren said.

"Yeah, not much of you is covered, buddy," Serena added.

"Sure, we don't wear a lot, but go-go dancing is a distinct type of dancing from stripping. Strippers, for one thing, end up completely naked, and we don't. Strippers sometimes have tassels on their nipples or butt cheeks. And most importantly, the style of dancing is different. We dance in a limited space, but we don't perform a strip-tease; those are the big differences between stripping and go-go danc-ing. Thank you for attending my lecture, the syllabus is outside," I joked.

"Oh, so like Magic Mike, that wasn't go-go dancing?" Serena asked.

"No, that was more like stripping, and it was more of a cabaret style," I said.

"And you said this is a bear night, right? I always get your gay subcategories mixed up. Which ones are the bears?" Lauren asked.

"Well, to be frank, your husband," I said, looking over at Brad.

"What did you say to me, punk?" Brad said, lifting his shirt to reveal his hairy stomach.

"I rest my case," I said, gesturing at his hairy body.

"What did you say?" said Brad, pretending to be offended.

"Nothing, just go have another drink with Mario," I said.

"Mario's already passed out in the guest bedroom," he said.

*Way to go, Mario.*

"Well, you're definitely not a bear," Lauren said.

"Yeah, you're like a twink or something, did I get that right?" Serena asked.

"For another couple of years, yes, I am," I said, as Serena giggled.

"So, how much are these people paying you?" Michelle asked, slightly concerned.

"I think I just get whatever tips I make, so I'm not sure yet," I said.

"Wait, you don't even get a base rate?" Michelle asked, even more concerned.

"No," I said.

"So, hypothetically, you could end up with five bucks at the end of the night?" Michelle asked pointedly, staring at me over her silver-rimmed glasses.

She wasn't at all out of line to ask that. I had not even considered the fact that, if no one tipped me at all, I could be doing all of this for free. In fact, I'd be operating at a loss because these outfits were cheap but not free. My mind was in such a desperate headspace when Jordy called me; I didn't even bargain or barter for a base rate. The thought didn't even cross my mind.

"Even if I only make five bucks, it's five bucks more than I have right now," I admitted.

Michelle pursed her lips and stared me down. I knew where she was coming from. Like a big sister, she didn't want her little brother to be taken advantage of or end up penniless. Nevertheless, I had no other choice but to proceed with the gig as planned.

"Well, one day we'll tell our little lima bean how Uncle DJ had a life before he settled down to become a rock star diplomat," Lauren said as she rubbed her stomach.

"Speaking of, I keep hearing that the lima bean has been kicking, but I haven't felt said kicking for myself yet. May I?" I inquired.

I started rubbing Lauren's stomach, unable to feel anything.

"Say hi to Uncle DJ," she said.

"Hi, Uncle DJ," I said, talking towards Lauren's stomach.

"No, I meant for the *baby* to say hi to Uncle DJ," she scolded jokingly.

"Oh, I'm sorry, you're telling your five-month-old fetus to say hello, and somehow *I'm* the crazy person here?" I joked back.

Flash, located in Fresno, was a bit of a drive from Lauren's house. The friends who remained at the party either had kids to put to bed or a blood alcohol content level too high to get behind the wheel. Unfortunately, this would be one performance of mine that this group of friends would have to miss.

Eventually, the straights began filing out one by one, and the clock struck eight: it was time to head over to Fresno. There are moments when I am anxious, and I need to just relax and listen to tranquil music to calm my soul: Mozart, Enya, and even Sinatra. Then there are other moments of anxiety when I need to just blast some crass, nasty club music and allow myself to cut loose. For this occasion, I chose the latter. Lots of Eminem, some Nicki Minaj, and the like. I got into my car, immediately blasted the heater, and scrolled through my playlists to find something to pump me up on my trip to Fresno. I selected a playlist, raised the volume louder than I normally did, and began driving.

The night was foggy, typical for late November in the Central Valley. As I journeyed through the dark country roads, my mind started to wander.

*You'll be fine. Don't freak out, there's nothing to worry about. No, you're going to be a disgrace. You can't dance; you know you're a horrible dancer. You could barely keep up with those fifth-grade girls when you were in middle school. Whatever, it'll be fine. I'm used to faking it. Fake it until you make it. Yeah, you're going to go viral, but for the wrong reasons.*

By the time I got to Fresno, I was relatively relaxed. I was only anxious over the fact that I *wasn't* on stage yet. I got out of my car in my wholesome Friendsgiving attire and began walking to the door. It was still very cold, so my walk turned into a brisk jog. By the time I was twenty or so feet away from the door, I was practically sprinting. I knocked on the door politely but emphatically. The person who had just entered the house opened the door for me, and there were several other guys in front of him taking their shoes off, too. None of them was Jordy, but I extended my hand and introduced myself to each of the guys.

I entered the kitchen, and there were a variety of drinks, both non-alcoholic and otherwise, covering the kitchen counters. Every person to whom I introduced myself was pleasant and handsome, but also big, beefy, and/or hairy; I stood out like a sore thumb.

Finally, I walked into a sort of den on the side of the house that was designated as the preparation room. And there he was. I saw Jordy talking to another dancer while rummaging through their respective garment bags. As soon as I made eye contact with Jordy, we both let out a little giggle. I rushed over to give him a big bear hug and brought my lips to his ear.

"I really hope they don't play Ease on Down the Road," I said.

Jordy howled his famous guffaw. He began cartoonishly slapping me on my shoulders before introducing me to another dancer, Max.

Max was the only one who was fully dressed in the Playboy-themed attire. He was wearing a sort of white leotard with a cotton tail on the lower back and a pair of bunny ears on his head. He reminded me of Elle Woods from *Legally Blonde* walking into a house party at Harvard after being tricked into thinking it was a costume party by a jealous classmate.

"How do I look?" Max asked us.

"Super cute! Except when I try to dress as a frigid bitch, I try not to look so constipated," I teased.

Since *Legally Blonde* is a classic and maintains a particular following among gay men, I had assumed that everyone in the room would get the reference and laugh. Well, the look this poor little bunny boy had on his face indicated that this was definitely **not** the case. Max, I would soon find out, had actually been homeschooled most of his life and had only somewhat recently come out. Therefore, he had not seen *Legally Blonde* and assumed that I was being completely serious.

*Nice going, jackass. Way to make a good first impression. Moron. The only skinny bitch in this entire entourage calling another boy constipated. Wow, just wow. This is why everyone hates you. No, it's ok. You just need to bounce back! No, you can't bounce back from that, dumbass.*

Thanks to Jordy's quick thinking and the influence he held with the other dancers, he immediately laughed it off and was able to defuse the situation.

"Oh my god, yes! Legally Blonde! I haven't seen that movie in forever. Maybe if we aren't too wasted when we get back, we can all watch it. It's one of the best. Movie night!" he screamed.

It took Max about four seconds to understand that I was just quoting a movie and trying to be playful, but boy oh boy, did I feel every single one of those excruciatingly long four seconds. I eventually apologized to Max, who accepted and explained to me that he had been homeschooled for most of his life and had not seen the movie yet. We ended the conversation by agreeing to watch *Legally Blonde* together someday, and that was that.

Once I was done doing damage control, I met Bob, the manager in charge of booking dancers and promoting the event. He was a very warm but professional gentleman in his 50s. He was, as were most of the other dancers, a bear. I extended my hand to greet him.

"Thank you very much for inviting me. I'm really excited for tonight," I said while shaking Bob's hand.

"We're excited to have you. Jordy tells me that the two of you did theater together?" Bob asked.

*Shit. He knows about my dancing skills. I bet Jordy told him about Ease on Down the Road and how stupid I looked. Did I complain a lot about my shin splints when I was younger? And if so, did Jordy relay that information to Bob? Don't be silly; he got you this gig. He must see something, or else they would have asked someone else, right?*

"Yeah, we've worked together on a few shows before," I said, intentionally avoiding the words dance, choreography, or klutz.

"Well, that's good to know. A lot of first-timers have problems with stage fright, but it doesn't sound like that'll be an issue with you," he said with a smile.

*It will not be.*

"Not at all! I love performing," I said.

"Perfect. So, a few things you should know. Our ride will be coming at 9:30 to transport you boys over to the club. We've split you all up into two groups, so you'll go in the second Caddy. You can pregame all you want; just be smart. Please don't be messy," he instructed.

"Of course," I said, wondering what past incident merited *that* warning.

"Also, I know you haven't danced like this before, so please no full nudity and don't ever let the customers do anything to you that makes you feel uncomfortable. If a customer makes you uncomfortable or tries to get up and dance with you, just make eye contact with the security guards; they'll be watching you boys at all times," he explained.

This made me feel nervous at first, but slowly reassured; the idea of being harassed at work had never occurred to me, but I was assured knowing that I had protectors.

"I appreciate that, thank you so much," I said.

"Anything else you need from me?" Bob said, indicating that I needed to get a move on.

"No, thank you so much for everything. I'll just be getting ready now," I said.

I snuck past Jordy on my way to suit up.

"Thanks for saving my ass," I muttered through my teeth.

"You're welcome, frigid bitch," Jordy responded, fighting back giggles.

Unzipping my gym bag and pulling out my outfit brought back the anxious feelings that I had felt when I had agreed to do this. I had my three outfits sprawled out on the couch. Staring at them for a while, I began to get nervous about being seen in them again. Choosing the most cautious option, I decided to put on the silky bathrobe and tight leather shorts. These shorts were very, very tight. I have no idea how Olivia Newton-John was able to fit into those long, tight leather pants at the end of *Grease*. I took a deep inhale and slid the black booty shorts up my long, hairy legs.

*This isn't happening. This isn't happening. Months ago, I would have thought I'd be working at a think tank or a university by now. What am I doing now? Putting on sexy leather pants and shaking my ass for dollar bills? Stop thinking about that, you're going to make a lot of money tonight. Be a slut and just have fun, goddammit.*

After getting dressed, the first SUV pulled into the driveway and took the first group away to the club. I meandered through the spacious home and found my way to the kitchen, where the remaining boys were standing by the countertop. One of the dancers asked if I wanted a shot.

"Sure, I'll take ten," I joked.

Some of the other boys wanted tequila, which I have duly nick-named the devil's piss, so I elected to drink my own liquor. I'm usually a vodka or whiskey drinker, but that night, I went with vodka. Those of us who were still in the kitchen all toasted to the late Hugh Hefner and downed our shots. The university I attended as an undergrad has a reputation for being a big party school, so while the other boys were wincing, sucking limes, or downing their chasers, I was helping myself to another shot. I'm *so* masculine.

The other boys insisted on doing another shot before we left, which I was fine with. I pounded the second shot and even made room for a third shot. I was starting to become tipsy, which loosened the tightness in my chest that had been building ever since Jordy asked me if I was interested in dancing.

After a few minutes, our carriage arrived. We all filed into the shiny, black Cadillac one by one and thankfully had plenty of space. This was a very high-quality SUV; the interior was black leather and practically spotless, it smelled like it was a brand-new car. I sat down next to Jordy to find that all the seats had already been heated by the seat warmer. I felt like a princess, albeit a slightly intoxicated princess.

The car pulled out of the driveway and headed for the club. Jordy leaned over to me.

"How are you feeling about tonight? Are you excited or nervous?" he asked attentively, rubbing my kneecap in a comforting manner.

"Girl, do you even know me?" I chuckled back.

Truth be told, I was not nervous at that point, per se. There just wasn't any precedent for this. I had no idea how crowded the club would be, what music would be played, how much money I would make, etc. Thankfully, with a few shots inside me to remove the edge, the butterflies in my stomach were temporarily numbed.

We were dropped off right at the front of the club, which had a very long line slithering out of it around the corner. We cut to the front of the line and wandered into the club with our garment bags. There were a lot of people, but the club was not quite crowded yet, as it was still relatively early. I followed behind Jordy closely as we meandered through the club like a maze. At the end of the club, there was a dressing room that was just big enough to accommodate all of us comfortably. The walls were bright neon green, literally a green room.

We all placed our gym bags of various sizes on the tables and began undressing again. Everyone had an outfit with a different style; some had plain black or white jockstraps and thongs, while others had bedazzled singlets. I looked over at the diversity of outfits and started comparing myself to everyone else. Most of the other dancers were wearing much more revealing outfits than I had planned on. At this point, I was in too deep to care. It was showtime.

Before I even put my trunks on, Jordy bumped into me.

"Hey, slut, did you bring a cock ring?" he asked very nonchalantly.

"Did I bring a *what?*" I asked.

"You know, one of those—"

"Yeah, I know what a cock ring is, I'm not *that* innocent. I'm sorry, no. I guess I didn't get the memo. Were we supposed to bring one?" I asked sheepishly.

"Oh, honey. If you want to make that coin, you've got to be willing to show off that big, pretty bulge that I know is in there. Most of us wear at least a cock ring," Jordy explained.

*At least? What the hell did he mean by at least? Never mind, you've seen Magic Mike over a hundred times. You know about the pumping scene.*

"Sorry, I don't have one," I responded.

"Here you go, Cinderella," Jordy said rolling his eyes playfully as he gave me his extra cock ring.

"Thank you, Fairy Godmother. If you save my ass one more time tonight, I swear to God, I'm going to be your kidney donor," I said graciously.

"Oh darling, if anything, I'm going to need a new liver," he said with a cackle that made me burst into laughter as well.

This was my very first time wearing a cock ring. I'm relatively hairy so putting the very tight silicon cock ring around my genitals was not the most comfortable sensation in the world. I stretched the ring as widely as I could and looped my very low-hanging balls into the ring first. Halfway there.

*Just one final piece of the puzzle, and there we go.*

Putting the very tight leather trunks on is what caused me the most pain. Strands of my pubic hair were pulled as I tried to place my bulge comfortably in front of the trunk. I placed the robe next, followed by the aviators, the sailor hat, and then the wooden pipe to complete the look.

After all of us were "dressed," we huddled together for a photo. I'm never camera-shy, but I was this time. The first potentially damning photo that could sink my future career working for the government was about to be taken. The boys around me did the sorority squat while others in the front turned their backs, facing the camera to show off their little cotton-tailed rear ends. I tipped my sailor hat downwards to cover more of my face and shoved the pipe in my mouth to obscure my face.

"Oh, look at all the cute little bunnies! You boys look fabulous. Let's go in one, two, three," Bob said as he snapped several photos from his smartphone. "We have about fifteen minutes, and then it's showtime. If you have to pee, please do it now."

As I would learn later on, it is typical for go-go dancers at most bars to work for thirty minutes straight and then take a thirty-minute break, but tonight was a little different. Because they were short on dancers, we were told the schedule would be closer to forty-five minutes on, ten minutes off.

My first position of the night was on a box up front near the entrance of the bar. Bob brought me back through the maze of the club that had just started to get a little bit busy. I noticed glances and a few double-takes from patrons at the bar. I began to overthink things again, but thankfully, I still had enough liquor in my system to ignore those thoughts.

When I reached my destination, I arrived at a black box set up near the wall between the entrance and the hallway to the other part of the bar. I stared at the box briefly, and my heart started beating faster and faster.

*Well. This is it. Time to dance.*

I got onto the box, took a very deep breath, and began dancing. I don't remember the music that was playing partly because I was trying my absolute utmost to stay on the damn box which was a lot harder than I thought. The box was probably only 20-25 inches in diameter, so it was tricky trying to move around, look sexy, and not be thrown off balance. I didn't have the bank account to go to the hospital.

My worries about getting unwanted attention or being photographed were put to rest in the first two minutes when I realized that there were not very many people in this part of the bar. There were a lot of people in line outside, but the security guards were letting them in at a snail's pace. I just grooved a little bit to the beat, not making any particularly ostentatious moves. Just shaking to the rhythm back and forth.

During the first five minutes, a couple of security guards at different times walked by and gave me a thumbs up, non-verbally asking me if I was feeling comfortable and safe. I responded with a thumbs up and a wink.

After what felt like ten minutes, I began to look around at the club patrons. It was nice to people watch, but after a while, the self-doubt reared its ugly head and brought back the horrible thoughts that I had tried to suppress. I felt myself sobering up from the shots, and so all the negative feelings that had been numbed were beginning to resurface.

*Is it going to be this slow all night? Did Bob post that photo he took of us in the green room? Are people commenting on it now? Are they asking why there is a tall skinny twink stuffed in the middle of a sea of bears? Are only bears going to be here, and if so, are they going to tip at all? Maybe that'll be to my benefit! I'll stand out, and maybe some of them will appreciate the fact that there is a single twink wedged in here! Who am I kidding? Bears almost always only go after bears; it's science!*

Just when I was beginning to doubt myself even more, two very giddy customers entered the club: Gavin and Damien. I tried to remain stoic as best I could, but it took so much not to break character. My friends began biting their lips and checking me out as the security guards checked their IDs and patted them down. After being scanned with the metal detector, Damien winked at me, then ran quickly out of sight while Gavin made his way towards me.

Whipping out some fresh dollar bills, Gavin looked at me with a slightly seductive gaze, which I immediately broke when I made a funny face back at him. He approached me at my box and looked up at me. He started massaging my calves seductively. I squatted down and thrust my bulge into his face a few times. I lowered my head down to his ear, talking loudly over the music.

"Well, here I am," I said, tipping my sailor hat.

"Ah, yes, here you are indeed. I think I've been a naughty little bunny," Gavin teased.

"Shut up, bitch!" I said, finally laughing. "Where did Damien go?"

"He's in the bathroom. I told him to go before we left, but as usual, he ignored me. An hour and fifteen minute car ride with a bladder full of piss is the karma he got," he said.

"Well, thank you for coming. I still don't know what I'm doing, but it's too late to go back now," I said.

Gavin placed his hands on me and squeezed my abs.

"You look hot. Own it, bitch," Gavin said with gusto. "Damien will catch up later. Now, I want my own personal little show."

Gavin had five one-dollar bills that he insisted on putting in my underwear one by one. The first bill started at my abs and slithered its way down to my happy trail before arriving at its final destination in my very tight waistband. Three of the other bills had a similar journey before he gave the gesture for me to spin around. I teased him a little bit by pretending that I didn't understand what he meant before winking and spinning around. He slid the dollar into the back of my waistband and smacked both of my cheeks, which, since I was wearing tight leather shorts, actually made a loud noise. Gavin winked at me and headed through the hallway into the club.

This was a good first start. A nice icebreaker and confidence booster, even though it was from a friend.

*You only got tipped because your friends feel bad for you. You're only going to get tipped by your friends tonight. Everyone else in the club is going to ignore you. Shut up; I'm fine. Everything is fine. Time to really sell it. This is only 15 minutes; has it been 15 minutes? I've lost track of time.*

A few more minutes went by before Enrique, who had also driven up a long distance to come support me, arrived with the same shit eating grin on his face. In our brief time as friends, he had been so supportive of me, as was the case this time when he brought a big fat 50-dollar bill and slid it into my trunks. I glared at him, non-verbally scolding him for giving me a tip that big. I wanted to make money, of course, but I knew how much Enrique made at his job on the campaign, and $50 felt like too much money. I repeated similar moves that I performed on Gavin and also got my cheeks slapped by Enrique.

After a few minutes, he winked at me proudly and then walked away giddily, sipping on his virgin Mai Tai.

After dancing for nearly an hour, I went on my first break. I should have known this coming into it, but I was very sweaty all over; there was not a single dry inch on my body. My hair looked and felt as though I had just climbed out of the shower. My body felt so sticky and gross; the other, more prepared boys had brought towels with them. I had not brought anything to dry my hair, so I snuck over to the bathroom next to the green room in an attempt to dry my hair with paper towels.

I popped open my water bottle and drank at least half of it in several large gulps. I shared my break with a very sweet dancer, who went by Z. Weirdly enough, Z struck up a conversation with me about comic books. While I do identify as a nerd, comic books are not the area of nerd-dom with which I identify. Nevertheless, I wanted to make friends with the other dancers, so I scraped the bottom of the barrel in my brain for anything that I possibly knew about comic books.

In the weeks to follow, I would learn that Z was a very accomplished go-go dancer and porn star. So accomplished in fact that when I googled him later on, I learned that he had won awards for, well, his work. He did not, however, brag about any of this. He didn't ask me if I had seen his work, nor did he bring up how many awards he had won. He didn't try to show me clips of him being in this porno or doing scenes with that star. He didn't brag about or count his tips, which were very clearly more abundant than mine. He didn't make me feel small or insignificant that entire night. All he cared about was who my favorite X-Men character was.

The perception among many people, including myself before this, is that adult performers, models, and/or go-go dancers are self-centered, egotistical, and mean. In just a few minutes of shooting the breeze with a very popular, albeit unknown to me at the time, go-go dancer, I learned that this was an inaccurate stereotype. Since then, I can honestly say I have never met a dancer who fits that profile. Ok, maybe there are a few exceptions; we're still human.

Things started to get busy as the clock ticked closer to midnight. This is when clubs traditionally see the heaviest inflow of patrons. By this point, I had only had one brief break backstage. There was sweat in every single crevice, every corner of my body. I could actually *feel* the saltiness in the sweat if that's even possible; I had never endured so much cardio in my life.

As the clock struck midnight, patrons in the club began to drink heavily and enjoy the vibe more. I moved to a different platform in the center of the dance floor that I shared with Max. Amidst the frivolity and loud music, as well as the smoke and mirrors, I gazed around the entire club. Everyone was lost in their own little world. Some people were making out passionately on the dance floor while others were glued to their phones. About a quarter of the patrons were either drunk or on some type of substance and just vibing hardcore with the music the DJ had been spinning. Very few people were looking at the dancers as colorful laser lights cut through synthetic fog in the club. I continued to scan the room, fighting to make eye contact with some-one, anyone.

I diverted my gaze directly to the back of the club and made eye contact with Damien. He had been watching me with the same look on his face that he had when he encouraged me to dance just a few weeks prior. I could never have imagined myself being there dancing at Flash without Damien's encouragement, and he knew it. I was very grateful for his insistence and the fact that he and Gavin drove over an hour just to come support me. Even more special was to have a friend like that with whom I needed no words to communicate. We were separated by a sea of people, but shared a connection deeper and stronger than anyone else in the club. I danced for the crowd, attempting to make eye contact with the patrons while occasionally looking over at Damien, who was looking at me like I was the only person in the room. After a while, he winked at me and raised his glass. I smiled, winked back, and then continued dancing for the rest of the club.

·  ·  ·

The dancers and I were driven back to the house around two in the morning. It was very late, and our bodies were exhausted from dancing the longer shifts. Super hungry, I randomly started craving curly fries with chicken nuggets. Bob and his partner graciously ordered us fast food. A nice Cadillac and now room service. Bon Appetit!

"I am so fucking stinky!" Jordy proclaimed as soon as we walked into the house.

"Yeah, you're glowing, sweetie," Max joked back.

"I'm so moist," Jordy exclaimed.

"Zip it, Judi Drench," I clapped back.

"Ok, that was funny, but fuck you!" Jordy sassed.

"I want to chop both of my legs off right now," Max complained.

"Well, I'm sure that stunning gentleman who couldn't keep his paws off you all night would be the first bidder at *that* auction," Jordy said, cackling.

"Ooo, you have a businessman lined up to sweep you off your feet, Pretty Woman?" I teased.

"Um, I have no idea what that means, but I think that Jordy is referring to a fat old, creepy closet case who doesn't miss a single bear night but always ignores me when we pass each other around town," Max lamented. "Stunning gentleman, my ass!"

*Well, I am just going to stop digging myself into a hole around Max. And no more movie references!*

"Yikes, I'm sorry to hear that," I said as I began disrobing from the evening.

"It's fine," Max said as he removed his pants and then took his jock strap off. "I don't go for straight married men anymore. Too much drama."

"You live for the drama, darling, don't lie to yourself," Jordy fired back as he got naked in the den.

"Well, yes. But also, I'm over it," Max said.

After disrobing into our comfortable sweatpants and hoodies, we all gathered in the living room, awaiting the healthy banquet that eventually arrived. Five very large bags of chicken nuggets entered the house, leaving an enticing aroma that brought the remaining boys from other parts of the house back into the living room.

We scarfed down the nuggets and fries like they were our last meals. We were starving and made no room for politeness or decorum.

"Who keeps burping? That's yucky!" Jordy screamed.

"Sorry," another dancer said right as he let out a very loud fart.

"Ew! No more! This is dinner time!" Jordy exclaimed.

"Sorry, I've been holding that one in all night," the dancer responded. "I didn't want to give anyone pink eye, so really, you should be thanking me for clenching."

"Well, clench a little longer, would you?" Jordy laughed as he chewed on his food.

As the food began to satisfy our ravenous appetites, we started eating more slowly. Then, the yawn train started making its way around the room. We all began chatting about the night, how many tips we made, etc. Then, out of the blue, Max looked down at his phone. Something he saw on his phone made his jaw drop immediately.

"Max?" Jordy asked.

Max didn't move a muscle.

"Max? Babe, what's wrong? Max?" Jordy insisted.

Looking up at us, with a sliver of a tear appearing in the bottom corner of his eye, Max let it out.

"There was a shooting tonight," Max said meekly.

"What? Oh my god, where? Here?" Jordy asked nervously as he reached for his phone.

"No, Colorado Springs. A nightclub. A gay nightclub," Max managed to get out as a tear began to stream down his right eye.

Sure enough, there had been a shooting at a gay club in Colorado Springs that very evening. All the merry vivacious laughter that had filled the room just a few seconds prior was instantly sucked out as we were all left in silence and shock.

As Americans, we are all used to hearing horrific stories of mass shootings rocking the country at least every month, if not every week.

As gay Americans, however, shootings that target our designated spaces affect us much differently.

*That very well could have been our bar tonight.*

Dead silence and creeping survivor's guilt began to fill the room. While our club had been full of loud music, dancing, and cute boys dressed as bunnies, another club only a few states away was wheeling out queer people, drag queens, and allies in body bags. This was a sobering reminder that the threat of violence against our community always lingers over our heads as we gather in our supposed safe spaces.

The last few minutes were a blur. After thanking both Bob and Jordy for the evening, I quickly got into my car and drove home. I drove home with very mixed feelings in my heart and very graphic images in my mind. On the one hand, I had just had the most spectacular night; I had danced the night away at my first go-go gig ever, boosted my self-esteem, and had a remarkable full-circle moment with my friend Jordy. Gavin, Damien, and Enrique had all driven over an hour just to come watch me perform. Not to mention, I made a little over $100 and enjoyed a delicious fattening meal with new friends. And yet, I could not for the life of me shake what I had just felt; dozens of parents in Colorado were about to get a phone call that would alter their lives forever. Meanwhile, I was driving home to my parents, who were comfortably sleeping in their beds and would wake up the next morning to see me.

I began to experience a feeling I hadn't felt often before: rage. Pure, white hot rage.

*Who the fuck is targeting our community and who the fuck do I need to fucking shoot?*

This was very unlike me, the angst was deep and personal. I didn't know how to get it out, so I began to speed up. I wanted nothing but to throw a brick through a goddamn wall.

*Innocent fucking patrons should be able to enjoy a night on the town without being fucking shot dead. God fucking dammit.*

I noticed that I was driving over 100 miles per hour. Thankfully, the logical side of my brain stepped in, and I realized that there were probably police officers out and about at that hour. I could not afford a ticket and definitely did not want to put myself, or another innocent driver, in harm's way.

The rest of my drive home left me feeling irresistibly pensive; even the sweetest of moments could turn bitter and heartbreaking within an instant. It's a lesson that I would continue to learn the hard way.

# CHAPTER 3

## S.O.S

I cannot definitively say that my night dancing at Flash was the last happy memory I had in 2022, but it was pretty much a tipping point, if anything else. Returning home later that night, my mixed feelings continued the following day when the details of the shooting began to be made public.

This was also not the first time I went out clubbing at a gay bar on the same night as a mass shooting. When I was a junior in college, just fresh off my 21st birthday, my friends and I went to a club in downtown Santa Barbara as a final celebration before we moved back home for the summer. When we returned from the clubs, sweaty, tipsy, and joyful, I scrolled through my phone before bed and saw something about a mass shooting in Orlando, Florida, but the details hadn't been released yet. Upon waking up the next morning, we learned that the mass shooting had been at a gay club in an apparent hate crime. The morning after dancing in Fresno brought me back to those same feelings of anger and survivor's guilt.

After dancing at Flash, I had assumed that the door would be open to dancing at future events, either with the bear night or possibly other events hosted by other promoters in Fresno. I followed up with Bob and some other people I met that night, but did not hear a response that day, which I thought was odd, but I didn't dig any deeper. As November turned to December, I followed up again with the promoters and didn't hear back again. This took me aback, but I assumed that everyone was just busy with holiday festivities.

*You weren't good enough. You didn't make the cut. Way to go, frigid bitch. You're not going to make any money ever. Nobody wants to hire you.*

For Christmas, I performed in a little holiday cabaret with Brad, Mario, and a few of our other theater friends. It was a great escape from the spiraling that had started to consume me more and more.

I started to drink more and more to drown out the negative thoughts. Drinking two to three shots before bed turned into three to four. Eventually, I was drinking five to six shots of straight vodka, bare minimum, and by that point, it was almost always by myself.

When it rains, it pours. As the calendar approached Christmas Day, things continued to go from bad to worse. The December bear event came and went, and I still had not heard back from Bob or anyone else. When I saw the advertisement for the December event on my social media feed, it felt pretty clear that I was not going to be booked again. I asked Jordy if he perhaps knew the reason or had any information on the selection process, which, of course, he did not. During this period, I also came down with a very severe sinus infection that sent me to the emergency room, desperate for air; it was the kind of cough that made you dry-heave. Worried it was COVID, I had to isolate myself, which worsened my feelings of despair.

As if being sick and not getting booked weren't bad enough, I started drinking more heavily than I had previously, which led to a falling out between me and Enrique. As a recovering alcoholic who had been sober for many years, Enrique could only tolerate so much drunk behavior. Our falling out was a gut punch to me that I was not in a good place and needed to correct course. But I didn't know what to do differently. The job rejections kept piling up, as did my fears about not being adequate for any kind of employment, dancing or otherwise. The ideal comfortable situation for me was being alone and drunk in a dark room listening to sad music. My philosophy is that when you can't look at the bright side, listen to "Mr. Brightside."

Being sick, unemployed, not booked, and with no end in sight, knocked my self-esteem to an all-time low. I was able to fake a positive attitude for most of December, but the energy to do that collapsed right after Christmas. This is where I began to truly spiral.

One particular evening in early January, I ended up drinking so much that I attempted video calling close friends and a few of my cousins. When the calls went to voicemail, I would send ominous-sounding messages. Late one night, which was when my negative feelings were usually at their worst, I began calling my friends nonstop until I heard an answer. The only one who picked up the phone that night was Gavin.

"DJ?" Gavin mumbled, very obviously half asleep.

"Hey, Gavin, can I just ask, do you hate me? Because Enrique hates me. I hate myself. Everyone hates me, so I just want to make sure that at least *you* don't hate me," I slurred out.

"Woah, ok, alright, what's going on? Are you ok?" Gavin asked.

*No, I am not fucking ok, Gavin. Who the hell would call you after midnight drunk as hell if everything was hunky dory?*

"No, I'm just chilling here. Chilling like a villain, that's me," I murmured.

"What are you talking about? Are you at home right now?" Gavin asked.

"Yes, I am. Home, sweet home. All by myself," I said. "I mean, I'm not alone."

I paused on the phone for a moment and started crying.

"You're not alone? Is someone there with you?" Gavin asked.

"Yes, indeed. Alcohol. Alcohol is with me," I slurred.

"Alcohol is with you?" he asked, confused.

"Yeah, I'm drunk," I slurred again.

"Yeah, I figured," he replied, trying but failing to mask his disappointment.

*Wow. What a bitch. He's also not wrong, I sound mucho loco.*

"That's right, buster. Alcohol is my best friend. And do you want to know why, Gavin? Alcohol is always there for you. Alcohol doesn't judge you. Alcohol doesn't ghost you, leave you on read, or make you feel like absolute trash. When you're the most lonely in the world, alcohol is a dependable companion," I said as I wept.

"Jesus Christ, DJ, calm down. People do love you. You're just having a bad night. We all love you so much. I'm so sorry you're going through this now. I wish I could be there to hug you, but unfortunately, I have a big event tomorrow that I have to wake up early for. Are you sure you're going to be ok?" Gavin asked.

"Yeah, no, do your thing. I'm sorry for pestering you, I'm sorry," I said, wiping the tears from my face.

"Ok, I love you, DJ, and so does Damien. Please be safe, ok? Can you promise me that?" Gavin asked.

"Yeah, no, I'll live. Me and good old Captain Jack," I said, referring to my half-empty whiskey bottle.

"Ok, I'll check on you in the morning," Gavin said. "Good night."

*There goes another one. You are such a goddamn leech on other people, do you know that? Are you noticing a pattern? Everyone ends up leaving you. Your exes, your old friends, your college friends, your new friends. Just fucking do it. You already know you have the thought; the question is, do you have the balls to do it?*

My pulse began to rush even higher, tears streamed down my face as I tried to drown out the negative thoughts with more swigs of alcohol.

*Do it. Fucking coward, do it. Nobody is going to miss you. Get the fuck out of my head, my family would miss me. Yeah, they're the only ones that you have left and even they are sick of your shit. You're such a goddamn disappointment. Loser. Do it. You know you want to. There are plenty of methods at your disposal. Find one and just do it fast.*

At this point, I had no actual method or plan. This was not a suicide attempt in the traditional sense. I was not going to prepare a note or even follow through with it at all. But I was done. I was desperate for help, and I didn't know how to properly ask for it. The effects of alcohol on my brain were also impairing my sense of logic; I was acting so out of character for me, or any logical person, for that matter.

Sending messages to friends wasn't enough. I wasn't hearing back from anyone. Logic would indicate that the reason I wasn't hearing back from people was because it was after midnight, but my depressed, intoxicated brain convinced itself that I was being intentionally ignored. As a result, I posted a series of cryptic messages on my social media stories. I don't remember the exact content of the messages. I do remember that they were not explicit, but they were very clear that I was in the danger zone, headed toward the deep end. This is arguably the most foolish thing I have ever done.

After a few minutes, I dozed off for a bit. I woke up and saw that I had over thirty missed calls from the same unknown number. Given how late it was and the fact that there were so many of them, I figured it was probably *not* a spam call.

Still lying down on my back, I called the number back.

"Hello, is this DJ?" a woman on the other line said.

"Yeah, who's this?" I said, barely intelligible.

"I'm calling from the county mental health services. I understand you're having a hard time tonight, is that right?" she asked.

Evidently, one of my friends saw my story and sent my cell phone number to a suicide hotline. I must reiterate that I was not suicidal. I did not have a plan, method, or note prepared. However, it was clear to at least one person that it was not out of the realm of possibilities.

"Oh yeah. My life sucks but it's no biggie. I'm just here chilling like a villain while everything merrily goes to shit," I mumbled with my eyes still closed.

"I hear you. I'm so sorry to hear that you feel that way. Well, some of your friends who love you said that you've been posting some things tonight on your social media pages, and they all want to help you," she said.

*Well, I guess I was wrong. One or two people don't want me to die. Huzzah.*

"No, I'm not going to hurt myself. I just want to stop feeling like this, but I probably will continue to feel like this forever, so it's just something I'm going to get used to. Don't worry about me," I slurred.

"Well, it sounds to me like a lot of people are worried about you," she said.

*A lot of people? How could she possibly know that? Sounds to me like one person saw my story and then thought I was going to do something irreversibly stupid.*

"That's nice of people," I said.

"Well, we need to make sure that you're going to be ok. If you need, we can send somebody over to your house to check in on you?" she offered.

Even in my intoxicated, depressed state, I knew perfectly well what that meant. She had the cops on standby and was ready to send them over. The thought of the police or even an ambulance arriving on my driveway and hauling my drunk ass off to God knows where sobered me up immediately.

"I'm really fine. I deleted the posts already, I'm just being stupid. I need to go drink some water and eat some carbs so I don't puke everywhere," I said, still slurring my words.

"Can you assure me that you are going to be ok? I need a verbal confirmation that you are going to be fine," she said.

"Yes, I am going to be fine," I said. "Thank you, suicide officer lady, ma'am."

"Alright. Our office provides a whole host of mental health services that I highly recommend checking out. Please know that you're not alone; there are people who love you and people who would love to help," she said.

*Right. She's clearly reading off goddamn script. She doesn't mean any of this. I bet she's made dozens of other calls like this tonight. I wonder what number I am.*

"Is there anything else I can do for you?" she said.

"Yes, actually. Who called you, and who gave you my number?" I asked.

There was a brief pause on the other line.

"We are not at liberty to disclose that information, sir," she said.

"Cool," I said. "Catch you on the down low."

"Goodnight, sir," she said.

Even before this phone call, I recognized full well the decline in my mental health. Each of these series of unfortunate events compounded each other: not being unemployed made me depressed, which made me want to drink more and shelter away, which worsened the depression and did not bring me closer to getting a job, which made me more depressed, and so on. This cycle felt like a treadmill; it's hard enough trying to keep up with the speed of the treadmill, but once you fall over, it's even harder to get back on. What's worse, I had felt compelled to pretend to be happy for friends and family over the holidays. Pretending for that long and suppressing what I had been feeling for so long made it so that when I finally let all the feelings out, I ended up passed out on the kitchen floor with multiple missed calls from a suicide hotline.

The rest of January was a vicious cycle of sadness, drinking, and being alone. I remember drinking pretty much every single night. My naturally extroverted personality does not do well when I'm alone, and since I had the house to myself for a large chunk of time, I had a lot of time to stew in the bad thoughts.

One night, I sat on my couch and started browsing through a certain hookup app. After scrolling through the same few profiles, I randomly received a message from a wealthy businessman who was staying the night in a hotel nearby. He was much older than me, but was very polite and respectful.

Speaking to someone new made me feel like my life was a clean slate, free from judgment. He knew nothing of how I had been feeling or how helpless I felt. All he was to me was an open ear with no knowledge of my tumultuous year, particularly the previous month. As we began chatting more, he indicated that he was just in town on business but would be returning to his home in Palm Springs the next morning. I had never been to Palm Springs, but as soon as he showed me photos of his home, my curiosity was piqued.

The house he lived in had a very nice pool and jacuzzi, an entertainment center, and a view of a fabulous golf course laden with the most massive palm trees I had ever seen. Suddenly, a thought popped into my head. We exchanged phone numbers. He was bored, and I was bored. Time for a phone call.

After chatting for over an hour or so, I boldly suggested the brain fart I had in my head.

"So, I know this sounds crazy, but all the best ideas in the world sounded crazy at first. I noticed that you have more than a few rooms in your home—"

"I'm going to stop you right there," he said.

*Crap, you overplayed your hand. Nice going, dumbass.*

"I actually was thinking of asking you the same thing. The thing is, I'm semi-retired, and I still do a lot of pro bono work with some non-profits in town, but I get lonely from time to time. If you're interested, you could stay in the master guestroom in the basement. I know we share an interest in the performing arts, so we could go see some on the weekends. If you need something to keep you busy, you could help me out in my rose garden," he said. "While you're here, I can take you to some networking events and introduce you to some people in town that could hook you up with a job."

As the conversation progressed, I felt the same sense of emotional whiplash that I had when Jordy asked me if I would dance at Flash. This was like a severe mutation of that. Never in a million years did I think this is where I would be at this point in my life, or ever. First, go-go dancing and now, living with a stranger in Palm Springs? What even is my life now?

I drank a little bit more whiskey and stared up at the ceiling, mindlessly listening to the conversation on the other end of the phone as the room began to spin around me. This idea was ridiculous, beyond ridiculous. But so what? Was there some wonderful opportunity elsewhere that I was giving up for this? Did I have anything to lose? Fuck no. If anything, I had a shot at maybe working on a campaign in Palm Springs, eventually.

*Just do it. Go to Palm Springs. That house is so stunning, you can just hang out skinny-dipping all day by the pool and get away from everything for a while. This dude seems like good people. He does a lot of good work in the community, so he's probably not a serial killer. This is your dream, this is what you've always wanted. No, this is another bad idea. Go-go dancing in Fresno didn't get you anywhere, so why do you think this will?*

Closing my eyes on the couch, I harkened back to a time when I was in graduate school. I had just finished a very stressful quarter, so stressful in fact that I did not even drive home for Thanksgiving because I didn't have enough time in between research, regular coursework, practicing Mandarin and Spanish, completing my thesis proposal, maintaining a rigorous workout schedule, and grading undergraduate papers. During that holiday break, I watched a news special about a serial killer who had a series of wealthy businessmen host him while he just traveled the world, stayed in luxury hotels, and flew first class.

That kind of life felt impossible for me. For one, despite my newfound feelings of rage, I had no intention of being a serial killer. In addition, I never thought of myself as physically attractive, so I assumed I would never be able to attract a man of that financial or social stature.

Well, here was an opportunity to live something that resembled what I had seen. To be sure, this would not be exactly like what I had seen in that news special, on either of our ends. He wouldn't be supporting me with lavish gifts and trips to Europe or the Caribbean. But what was the point of saying no? I would have the chance to relax and reset in the sunshine, see some good theater, and maybe network with whatever connections this guy had.

*Do it. You've got nothing to lose.*

"I'm in. I'll see you in a week," I said, and then immediately ended the call.

A few days before I left for Palm Springs, Brad and Lauren hosted a Super Bowl party at their house. I decided to reveal my Palm Springs plan to my friends there. I had no idea how they would react, and honestly, I didn't even care. The only thing that mattered was that I had made my decision, and they needed to know it.

I managed to sneak Lauren and Michelle away from the TV, and we talked at the kitchen table about what I was planning to do.

"So, you've never even met this guy? You're just going to pack up and move to Palm Springs. Do I have that right?" Michelle asked.

"Yes, ma'am, that's right," I said, unfazed by the tone of her voice.

"So—" Michelle said, at a loss for words, "is that the long-term goal?"

"I don't really have much of a long-term goal, and I really don't care at this point," I said.

"Why don't you just apply to a job for a politician who focuses on Asia?" Michelle asked.

*Well, by golly, Michelle. That's a great fucking idea. I sure wish I had thought of that before! I guess I should go and do that. Oh, wait a second, I've already done that several fucking times and have been railroaded at every goddamn turn!*

"Been there. Done that," I said, abrasively. "Everyone who finally does get back to me several months later gives me a big fat no, and I'm sorry, but I'm done applying to stupid places online."

"Well, you would think with your background, you would be getting a lot of offers," she said.

*You. Would. Think.*

"What about being the interim manager at the theater here in town? We've been interviewing candidates, but probably won't find a full-time manager for a few more months, so you could just do that. It wouldn't pay much, but it's something, and you wouldn't have to commit full-time," Lauren suggested.

"And be stuck here in town and never be able to leave? I need to try something brand new out of this valley. A little patchwork of a part-time job isn't going to help me. I need to get far away from here. I think this is a great idea, and I've got nothing to lose. I just want to throw some spaghetti at the walls and see what happens. I think it's genius," I said. "And even if it's not genius, it's better than being stuck here."

Lauren and Michelle both looked at each other and then back at me very disapprovingly. As I stated earlier, I had looked up to them as my big sisters, and they had always treated me like their little brother. This encounter, however, felt much more like I was Huckleberry Finn being given a talking-to by the Widow Douglas and Miss Watson.

"DJ, what're you doing?" Lauren asked.

"Sitting here, sipping on a cocktail, chatting with you ladies, why?"
I said.

"Yeah, you've been enjoying a lot of cocktails recently, haven't you?
How many have you had?" Michelle asked sternly.

"I'm not sure. I stopped counting after the first quarter," I joked.
Lauren and Michelle exchanged disappointed looks again. "This is my
first one. I was joking. I just look messier than I am."

It's true. I hadn't been shaving, trimming my nails, or grooming
myself very much those months. I had only showered that day because
I knew I'd be around people.

"I think you should drink some water," Michelle said calmly.

"Fine," I said, getting up to get some water before returning to the
table.

"Do whatever you need to do, we won't stop you. But please know
that your niece or nephew will need Uncle DJ around, so just please
take care of yourself," Lauren said as she placed both hands on her
stomach. I avoided eye contact as I drank water and finished my slice
of pizza, fully disassociating from the conversation.

A couple of hours later, the game ended, and my friends each
determined I was able to drive. Recognizing that their fears had not
been calmed, I promised that I would share my location with them
and call them if anything bad happened. I could tell they were disappointed in me, but I didn't care. I needed to break the cycle of being
sad, lonely, and drinking by myself every evening.

On the drive home, I felt unhappy. I drove with my hands firmly
gripping the wheel. My road rage was higher than normal that day. I
honked, screamed, and tailgated several cars. I could feel my rage
building up to the point it had when I drove home from Flash. It
reminded me of all the horrors that happened that night. The
thoughts of members of my community being wheeled out in
stretchers and heading for the morgue returned and filled me with
rage. The camaraderie of being around the other dancers was the one
thing that had comforted me that night, and now, two months after
not seeing those boys again, I felt like I didn't even have that. I felt
alone with nothing but my negative thoughts and my newfound rage.

Suddenly, I received a phone call. This time, it was from Enrique.

"Hello?" I asked.

"Hey there," Enrique said warmly.

"Hey, Enrique," I said.

"What's up?" he asked.

*What's up? Seriously? Last time you saw me I was drunk off my ass, you do the math.*

"Nothing, I'm just driving back from a Super Bowl party," I said, hiding my annoyance.

"Well, that sounds fun. Did your team win?" Enrique asked sarcastically. He knew I didn't have "a team." This was classic Enrique teasing.

"No, but I liked the halftime show," I said, trying to keep my answers brief.

"I see, I see. Well, I'm calling because I have some news to share with you, and I wanted to share it with you in person if you were available sometime tonight," he said.

*Well, what a coincidence, Enrique. I have some exciting life developments to share with you as well.*

"Tonight?" I asked.

"Yes, either tonight or tomorrow at the latest," he said.

This sounded urgent. I figured he was going on a trip or something because Enrique was always very flexible when he wanted to meet up. Issuing a deadline was out of character for him.

"Yeah, I have some time now," I said.

"Ok, cool. You want to meet at the Thai restaurant by the old campaign office?" he asked.

"Sure, I'm just heading south now. I should be there in about half an hour," I said.

"Awesome! I am looking forward to it," he said, very upbeat.

"Me too, I'll see you soon," I said before immediately hanging up the phone.

To say that I was relieved would be an understatement. I was extremely hurt when Enrique stopped talking to me, but I was also perfectly understanding as to why he did. Not long after we had become friends, he told me story after story about his struggles with alcoholism and his road to recovery. He didn't mind me getting drunk; he even bought me drinks from time to time and loved it when I sent him funny videos of me saying weird things while I was drunk. But the night he stopped talking to me, I knew I had crossed a line and that I was completely at fault. The fact that he reached out and wanted to talk, presumably to make amends, made me breathe a deep sigh of relief.

I arrived at the restaurant around seven. During the grueling weeks of the campaign, Enrique and I would pig out at this same Thai restaurant. I would always order the same thing, yellow curry, while he would change his order. He would order vegetarian spring rolls for us to share and always picked up the check.

Walking into the restaurant, I felt nervous. There was not much I was expecting other than to talk about what had happened and how we could hopefully patch our relationship up. I found Enrique sitting at the same booth that we always loved to sit at. This, I hoped, was a sign that he was as eager as I was to be friends again.

We hugged, and Enrique indicated that he had already ordered for both of us. We made small talk before chatting for a bit about politics, the contentious battle for Speaker of the House, and a lot of other stuff that deeply interested both of us but would probably bore 98% of everyone else. Then we started to talk about our friendship breakup.

"I don't want to revisit everything that happened that night other than to say that I was really disappointed in you," Enrique said, looking directly into my eyes and not even blinking.

"I know," I said, fighting back tears.

"I can't judge. I won't judge. I'm sober, but I'm still an alcoholic. I'm not saying you are; that's not why I'm here. All I wanted to say is that I love you," he said.

There was a very long pause. We stared into each other's eyes for what felt like an hour. I knew perfectly well what he meant. This was not a romantic confession. Enrique and I were close and had very similar interests, but we were not at all romantically attracted to one another. I was fighting back tears, but could not hold back any longer.

I put my face in my hands and began sobbing intensely. I knew this would annoy him; Enrique came from a family and culture where crying was not a thing for men. After I pulled myself together to get the napkin he was handing over to me, I started to breathe deeply.

"I know. And I love you too. That's why I was so upset not to hear back from you for a month. And I know I take the full blame for everything that happened, but I think you should know this," I said, trying to stop crying again. "That night after you left, I drank even more. I know that's hard to believe. But I did. And..."

This was the part I had the hardest time holding it together.

"And, I started posting stuff on my social media profiles which, long story short, led to one friend calling an emergency hotline because he, or she, thought I was going to kill myself," I said as I continued to weep.

Enrique looked shocked. I'm not sure he had fully grasped the mental state I was in. My pain was much more than just being down on my luck from a job; the pain was rooted in not having a purpose, direction, or hope. He just stared at me in disbelief.

"Well, I—" Enrique said, trying to find the words.

"It's ok, you don't need to say any more. I fucked up. I know I fucked up. Everything that happened was my fault. I just wanted you to know," I said earnestly.

He reached out and held my hand tightly. I started crying harder.

"I want you to take better care of yourself. I love it when you're a little bit silly and you send me those cute little videos. But I hope you start moderating your drinking while I'm gone," he said.

My crying stopped.

"While you're gone?" I asked, sniffing and wiping away tears.

"Well," Enrique's face brightened up slightly, "I wanted to tell you that I got a new job! It's in Denver."

"Oh, Denver?" I asked, still in a bit of shock.

"Yeah, I've never done local government work before, but there's a first time for everything! I'll have to drive my ass all the way out there, but I'm looking forward to starting something new. Nobody in the party here is answering my calls or applications," he said.

*Join the club, dude.*

"Oh, that's great," I said, trying my best to look supportive and also mask my sadness for him leaving. Just as Enrique was coming back into my life, he was leaving for another state halfway across the country.

"You'd better come visit. I know you have family out there, so I hope you stop by if you'd better come and say hey," he said.

"Yeah. My friend Jake lives there and I'll be there this summer for my cousin Kiana's wedding, as a matter of fact," I said.

"Oh, yeah? Are you going to be the stripper at the bachelorette party?" Enrique asked, with a sarcastic blank expression on his face.

We broke into laughter, and with that, the tension broke. It was almost like the past month of not speaking to each other had never happened. With all the bullshit, stress, anger, and feelings of hopelessness I had endured, it felt good to at least have one of my best friends back. I knew that he did not mean to hurt me; he drove all the way to Fresno to tip me $50 for crying out loud.

"So, what have you been up to?" Enrique asked inquisitively.

I told him all about Palm Springs and my plan to move out there. He was a lot less concerned about it than Lauren and Michelle were, specifically because I was holding out on the hope that I could lock in a job for a campaign out there. Enrique told me he would make as many calls as he could to see if he knew anyone who worked in the area who might get me a job. I knew he was in my corner, as he always had been, and as he always would be.

When our food came, we chatted more about politics, Enrique's move to Denver, and mine to Palm Springs. After we finished our food, Enrique grabbed the check, walked me back to my car, and gave me the longest goodbye hug.

"You're going to be fine. And if you aren't, you have my number," he whispered into my ear.

I got back into my car, fighting tears, and made my way back home. Enrique, who did not even have a college degree, let alone a master's degree, had secured a job based largely on his positive attitude and incomparable work ethic. I aspired to be the same way, but given my state of mind, it felt like an uphill climb.

As much as I tried to emulate some of Enrique's best qualities, it felt nearly impossible to be positive. Against his wishes, I did not moderate my drinking. I began drinking almost always alone. Gavin and Damien were among the very few friends I had in town. They did not hang out with me as frequently due to both of their job situations, but my stupid, depressed brain forced me to think that this was my fault.

*See? Not even your close friends want to hang out with you. You're alone for a reason, it's because you're such a goddamn disappointment to literally everybody.*

I remember waking up the next morning, scrolling through social media, and getting it into my head that I would be lonely and miserable forever. I convinced myself that everyone was only socializing with me to humor me or because they felt bad.

Sensing how distraught I felt, my mom took me out for a drive that afternoon. Several family members had endured some level of mental health distress over the previous three years, so long car rides became our emotional releases. The weather that day, I remember vividly, was super bizarre. The sun was brighter than normal but was concealed behind a barrage of dark, eerie-looking clouds. The Sierra Nevada Mountains were snowcapped and stunning as usual to provide a landscape to drive into. And then it started to hail.

*How cliché.*

I finally told her what I was doing when I "went out" to Fresno to dance for the first time. Then, I told her my Palm Springs plan. That took a lot of pressure off the go-go dancing confession. She was extremely alarmed. My mother, bless her heart, is naturally a very anxious person, so this brought her anxiety to new heights.

"And you've never even met this person?" she asked.

"Nope," I said, not expressing any emotion whatsoever.

"And you're planning to live with him?" she asked.

"Yup," I said, maintaining the same careless attitude.

"And, how long are you planning to stay there, and what is your game plan?" she asked.

"I plan to go to Palm Springs, detox, and figure things out while I'm there," I said.

"So you plan to go to Palm Springs, live with a complete stranger at his house, and just wing it?" she asked, trying to make the idea sound as absurd as it was.

"Yup," I said.

"Ok, sweetie, are you able to see the multiple red flags here? Like, at all?" she asked, very concerned.

I didn't respond. I just looked forward and shrugged my shoulders. Looking out the window, I looked around at the scenery and acted as though my mother were not even there.

The rest of the car ride was silent. I could tell my mom was feeling a combination of disappointment and fear. Being her last-born, I was always treated as the youngest even into adulthood. Our journey ended at the ice cream shop where my mom got out of the car and ordered me two scoops of one of my greatest weaknesses: mint chocolate chip. Ice cream, and particularly that flavor, had always made me feel better; not this time. I grumpily licked my two scoops as we headed home. I could only taste the texture of the ice cream, not the flavor. Every little frozen granule felt rough on my tongue, but the flavor remained elusive. I was not able to taste the savory goodness of one of my favorite desserts.

When we returned home, I got ready to pack for my indefinite trip to Palm Springs. Walking back into my room, I started to tear up as I packed my two suitcases. I packed a variety of clothes for all types of weather because I had no idea how long I would be there or even if I would ever come back home. I glared at the frames holding my useless diplomas on the wall next to the framed photos of my time abroad. Feeling cynical and bitter, I packed even faster. I needed to get the hell out of Visalia.

I walked back into the kitchen to pack some snacks. My parents were standing there next to each other, looking deeply concerned. It looked like my mother had been crying, which I always hate to see. My dad looked equally distraught. I paused for a moment, looking at them. Trying my best to look confident, I even tried forcing a smile, which lasted about five seconds. I then collapsed onto the kitchen floor and began hyperventilating.

I cried my eyes out, feeling as helpless as ever. My poor, sweet, loving parents, both of whom have arthritis, got down with me on the floor as I cried. My mom even started crying with me, too. They had always said they were so proud of my accomplishments and were by far my greatest cheerleaders throughout my life. I really could not think of anyone more supportive than my parents. And now, here they were, huddled around me on the kitchen floor as I vented my anger and frustration.

"I have to do this, I have no other choice, I'm so done feeling useless," I said several times in a row.

"You're not useless at all, DJ. Not at all," she said.

"This is just an endless cycle of the fuck you game. And why? What have I done wrong? I played by the rules. I got an education from two great universities. I speak three goddamn languages. I am a good public speaker. I'm funny, in fact, I'm fucking hilarious. I'm smart. But then again, maybe I'm not. If I were really that fucking swell, I'd have offers out the door and around the corner. I guess employers are sensing that I ain't shit," I ranted.

"I really don't like it when you use those words, and especially don't like to hear you talk badly about yourself," she said calmly.

"Well I really don't like it when businesses and politicians make me write full fucking cover letters when I apply to work for them and then I don't even get a goddamn courtesy email back," I said angrily through my teeth.

"I know, that's been frustrating, and not very professional at all," she said, trying to console me while also showing her dislike for my foul language.

"And this town is just so lonely. I have like three friends, and they all have busy lives. I feel like such a burden on everyone," I said.

"We are telling you, you aren't a burden at all," she repeated. "You know your family loves you. But your cousins are starting to worry about you."

"How do you know that?" I asked.

As I would learn a few months later, my two closest cousins, Kiana and Kristen, had created a group chat with my mom. They would share information: Kiana and Kristen would report what they had seen on my social media feeds, and my mom would describe what she was seeing at home. I would later grow to appreciate this, but at the time, it made me even more paranoid and distrustful.

"They just want you to be happy," my mom said, attempting to divert the conversation away from further scrutiny.

"I just thought I had all these skills and that someone would care by now," I said.

"We know! You just haven't found where you're meant to be yet," my mom said, rubbing my back.

"Well, it seems pretty clear to me that I'm the problem. I'm getting rejected from every single place I apply to. My friends have jobs, my cousins have jobs, and a lot of my graduate cohort found jobs. I must be the problem. I'm clearly the common denominator," I said.

"It certainly feels that way now, doesn't it?" she said.

"And do you want to know what the worst part is?" I said. "All I'm trying to do, all I want to do, is make the world a happier, better place. The world just doesn't seem to want me to be happy."

"It certainly feels that way, now," she repeated.

They continued to hold me for another ten minutes before we all got up and headed over to the couch. Both of them were still incredibly worried about my state of mind, but also saw that I was not budging; the more they pushed back, the more it emboldened me. I was going to go to Palm Springs, come hell or high water. Their only requests were that I turn my location on, book a virtual session with my therapist, and update them at least every two days.

I wiped off the tears from my face and started to pack the luggage in my car. My mother was fighting back tears as she hugged me, as was I. As was the case a few months before, I had made my decision and was not going back. With my baggage all packed, I hopped into the driver's seat and started driving. Palm Springs, or bust.

# CHAPTER 4

## ALMOST PARADISE

The weather was quite ominous when I drove down to Palm Springs that night; the cold, rainy front from the day spilled into the night. It started pouring heavily, so heavily that I set my windshield wipers to the maximum level. As the rain continued to descend, a million thoughts swirled in my head. Fortunately, there were so many of them that they seemed to cancel themselves out.

*This will be great for you. You will end up on the six o'clock news. This is your chance to work for a campaign! They're going to find you in the basement naked upside down. Etc.*

As I made my way down south, I randomly got a call from a college friend of mine, Will. While he was a few years older, we had quite a few classes and participated in our college choir together. He was always a decent guy and very fun to be around. Both of us had a very similar, quirky sense of humor. Having not heard from him in a while since he got married and had three kids, it was a pleasant surprise to hear from him out of the blue. We exchanged niceties before he got down to brass tacks.

"I need your honest opinion about something. Please don't hold back; tell me exactly what you think about this idea," Will asked.

"You know I never filter my thoughts," I joked.

"Of course. Well, here goes: I am planning to run for local office, and I wanted to ask you what your thoughts were. I know you've volunteered on several campaigns before, so you know a little bit about how things work. I am completely new to this, so this is sort of uncharted territory for me," he said.

I proceeded to ask him about his motivations for running for office, which were largely because he had three daughters and was concerned about the world that elected leaders were creating for them and their futures. We talked about the different ways to get started with campaigns, the networking that is required, and the stamina needed for running for office. For about a good solid hour, we discussed so much about politics before the conversation drifted over to my life.

"So, when are *you* going to run for office?" Will asked.

*Holy shit. What a box of bricks to hit me with. Does he know what I've been doing for the past nine months? I guess he doesn't know about the go-go dancing, much less what I am doing right this second.*

Will and I went in different directions after college. We both graduated the same year with very ambitious plans. I went away to explore language learning and graduate work, but had now fallen flat, to put it nicely. Will, on the other hand, had gotten married, started a family, found stable employment as a music instructor, and had the foundation to build a successful career in politics. He had more of a firm foundation upon which to build a career in politics; I did not.

"Well, I have a lot to catch you up on, dude. I'll be in the car for at least another couple of hours. If your kids are asleep or you have nothing better to do right now, buckle up," I said.

"Sure, man. What's been going on?" Will asked intently.

That's what I loved about Will. He had a gay younger brother, so he was very comfortable discussing a wide variety of taboo topics. While he was straight as an arrow, he had enough of an open mind and compassion for me to be real with him. We hadn't seen each other in a very long time, but I sped up to the more recent nine months. I told him about go-go dancing at Flash, which he, of course, had been to.

"No way, dude! Why didn't you tell us? We would have totally come out to watch you!" Will exclaimed.

"Yeah, well, it's all still pretty new to me, so the people that came were primarily gay people. I told some straight people about it, but it's still pretty new to me, so I'm not sure who is comfortable with it and who isn't," I said.

"Listen, dude, do you want to know what my first night at Flash was like?" he asked.

*Oh god. So much to unpack here. First of all, yes, I absolutely want to hear what your first night at Flash was like. And secondly, your **first** time at Flash?? There was a second and a third or more? Oh my god, Will. Spill!*

"Sure!" I said, trying my best but probably failing to contain my excitement.

"Ok, well, my brother invited me out to Flash a couple of years ago, and so a few of the guys from choir went out and, unbeknownst to us, my brother's boyfriend was dancing that night. I had only met him a handful of times and then all of a sudden *bam* I see my brother's boyfriend's sweaty ass cheeks twerking up on stage in a leather thong. I was fine with it eventually, but I just wasn't ready to see that particular person's booty cheeks. So, in summary, that was my first experience at Flash, so anything else you say will probably not shock me," Will said.

*Hold my beer.*

I told him about my spiraling descent and spending many nights, particularly the previous few hours, crying on the kitchen floor. And then, I held no punches when I told him what I was on my way to do.

"So, you've never met this guy?" Will said.

Ok, maybe it's not just my mom and my friends. This started to feel like a straight versus gay thing. For gay men, meeting up with strangers for hookups or even platonic encounters was not weird at all.

"Yeah, dude. I'm ready to just throw as much spaghetti at the walls and see what sticks. I really can't go back to feeling the way I did last month or even last night. There's just no end in sight, so I need to set my sights on something else," I said.

"So, does that mean that you don't want to pursue politics or public policy anymore?" he asked.

This was a very hard question to hear. It had been lingering in the back of my mind for most of the last few months, but hearing it verbalized in such a blunt manner gave me pause.

"Hello? Are you still there? Did I lose you?" Will asked.

"I'm thinking," I responded.

In all honesty, the idealized vision that I once had for my future was getting blurrier by the second. Perhaps the stress I had experienced over the past nine months was due to having a supposedly clear picture of the direction where I was headed, then beating myself up when I didn't feel I was on track. It was in this question that I realized I was not just wandering off from my intended path but rather floating through space without any direction at all.

"I don't know, dude. I need money right now, and I'm sure as hell not getting it for using my brain. I feel so disillusioned by everything, which I guess is a good first step for going into that business, but honestly, it's been so stressful trying to be something instead of just trying to be me, if that makes any sense to you at all," I said.

"Damn. Well, you would think with your skills and stuff that you'd be the first one to be hired somewhere," he said.

*Oh. My. God. If. I. Hear. That. Sentence. One. More. Time. I. Am. Going. To. Scream.*

"It's just not doing it for me now. The resume doesn't seem to be getting me anywhere," I said. "So I'm just letting life take me where it will and go from there."

"No, I get that, homie. I've definitely been where you are right now. I thought I would be single forever until I met Hannah. I didn't picture the life I had when I was your age, so no pressure at all, dude. You're a really awesome guy, and you're going to land somewhere," Will said.

After the episode I'd had on the kitchen floor just a few hours earlier, this was a relieving thing to hear. No judgment, no phoniness, just someone who knew me personally giving an objective assessment of his experience and delivering a hopeful message to me as I entered uncharted territory. I was still very uncertain about what the following trip would entail, but I eventually calmed down thanks to Will's kind words.

Still, the kindness Will showed me during that call did not tame the existential fears I had in my head. He was married, with kids, and ready to start on a new career in a field I had wanted to break into. The rest of our college classmates, as we continued to reflect, were also kicking ass. They were all getting married, having kids, buying homes, and starting their careers. One of our classmates who was in the choir with us even ended up as a dancer on Broadway. *He*, I must note, was an actual triple threat. It felt good to reminisce together about old times and old friends, but it was beginning to make me feel small. We chatted for the rest of my journey up until I approached the city limits of Palm Springs.

"You have my number, don't hesitate to use it," Will said.

"Thank you so much. Good night, Will. Love you, dude," I said before ending the call.

I pulled into the driveway and turned my car off. The sky itself was black as could be, but since the house was far removed from the rest of the city, I could see the moon beaming down brightly, surrounded by stars that were more visible to the naked eye. I walked up to the front door, too tired and unmotivated to be anxious. All I wanted to do was fall asleep and begin the reset process.

After a few minutes of waiting, my host opened the door. He was much shorter than I and giddy as could be, not exactly the profile you'd expect from a serial killer. I was greeted with a hug and a helping hand to get my luggage inside.

Walking into the home where I would be staying indefinitely, I can't say I had a single ounce of worry in my body. The interior of the home was gorgeous, very clean, and rather spacious. Fine art covered the walls while massive glass windows surrounded the mid-century modern living room.

My host led me downstairs to what felt like a basement. As soon as I reached the bottom of the stairs, I tried not to let my jaw drop to the floor. There was a massive entertainment center, clad with books and records all around it. The flat screen was well over 80 inches and was surrounded on either side by very large speakers.

We continued walking into what would be my bedroom. The room was not as large as the living/entertainment room but had a very comfortable queen-sized bed and windows that, I would learn the next morning, faced the golf course outside. We chatted for a little while about our plans for the week before my host kept noticing my repeated yawning and took his cue to let me rest. He went back up to his room in a separate wing of the house, and I began to get ready to sleep.

I went to bed that night feeling not uncomfortable, per se, but maybe slightly uneasy. No doubt, I had gotten used to moving to different places over the years, but this wasn't the same. I had moved away to college, graduate school, and several foreign countries, but each of those journeys was all for the purpose of achieving something, even if the particular end goal wasn't clear. This was completely new. I had no real game plan other than maybe have a shot at working in politics down here, and even that didn't feel like a done deal. I attempted to sleep off any negative thoughts or regrets about my decision, about which there were many.

Waking up the next morning felt like a fever dream. The views were even more stunning than the photos had indicated. Since it was early March, the mountains were still snowcapped, and the grass that covered them was particularly luscious and green. I took a tour of the empty house and got a fantastic view of both sides of the house. The golf course was huge and stretched in either direction. Retired golfers and their young caddies whizzed around in their golf carts.

The crystal blue pool was massive, and the connecting hot tub was bursting with jet-powered bubbles. The patio had several reclining lounge chairs lined under pool umbrellas. There was an outdoor barbecue and kitchen with a completely stocked refrigerator. It looked like the kind of yard that you would find in a lifestyle magazine.

My host left that afternoon to run some errands. Elated that I had a massive house to myself for a few hours, I stripped naked and began snapping photos of myself everywhere. Inside the house, outside the house, by the pool, with the golf course in the background, in the kitchen, etc. It was a somewhat liberating feeling as though I had a truly blank slate to start over again, and having *this* kind of blank slate was perfectly fine with me. The first morning brought me a sense of cautious optimism that this move was going to be good for me, both professionally and personally.

My host and I went to the theater in L.A. the first weekend after I arrived. The weekend was very cold and rainy, typical for early March in Southern California. We arrived at our very ritzy hotel in downtown L.A. sometime in the afternoon. Our room had two queen-sized beds for each of us. Trying to maintain an open mind, I decided to enjoy myself that weekend and not dwell too much on job opportunities, networking, or resumes. I loved the theater, and so I dedicated my attention to that.

Once we began attending some of the pre-show events and parties together, I started to feel a little bit uncomfortable. I always feel at ease in social settings, but that is only when I am confident in who I am or who I am with. Talking to wealthy, artsy patrons about where I was from or, even more awkward, who I was and who I came with were much more difficult questions to answer.

*Do I call him my friend? My confidant? Acquaintance? Do we lie and say that we're related? He looks nothing like me, nobody is going to buy that. They must know we have separate bedrooms, right? Right?*

Matters became even more uncomfortable when I started analyzing people's facial reactions. People would look at me, then look at my host, and then non-verbally communicate that they "got it." But did they?

The attempt to enjoy myself was off to a weak start. I couldn't shake this feeling off. I felt like I was walking through a landmine when people asked me about my current living situation, not wanting to say the wrong thing to invite further scrutiny or, even worse, judgment.

To defuse the discomfort, I resorted to my favored defense mechanism, humor. Sipping on a few glasses of ridiculously-priced champagne, I started telling funny stories about my time abroad, particularly my post-graduate European trip. Thankfully, everyone else was drinking too, so the nerves and tension all around went down.

The show was very long but enjoyable, thanks in part to the glasses of champagne in the founder's room. And yet, being surrounded by so much luxury did not insulate me from more negative intrusive thoughts.

*You're Pretty Woman. They even went to a damn show together in the movie. Shut up, we're just friends. That's what we are. I'm a friend going to the theater with another friend. Who cares what people think?*

Time went on, and I started going to events with or without my host. I should have expected this, but since Palm Springs was largely a retirement destination, I was often the youngest person in the room by far. Every time I tried to steer the conversation to something about my possible employment prospects, I could notice the eyes of most of the men leering down at my body and not paying very much attention to what I was saying. This is flattering, please understand this. It's not like I don't like being complimented on the body I have worked so hard on. The problem is, I felt as though I worked too hard to achieve a whole host of other skills that I felt like were going unseen.

It was time to redirect strategies. Maybe, just maybe, I could take advantage of my looks to get myself *into* social functions and networking events in a city like Palm Springs. Once I was safely in, I could show off my polished resume as well as my prowess for public speaking and working a room. If employers or recruiters saw just how ambitious I was, maybe I could break through in a way that I could not when I applied for jobs online.

One weekend when my host was out of town on business, I decided to attend a high-end networking mixer in Cathedral City, a hop, skip, and a jump away from the city of Palm Springs itself. My suit was ready, my elevator pitch memorized, and my hopes cautiously optimistic.

The mixer was held early in the afternoon at a gated golf course with a large country club situated in the middle. To give you an idea of how ritzy this place was, I'm pretty sure my car was the only non-electric and the only model there that came out before 2020. I parked my dusty used car in the parking lot with a view of a massive pond adjacent to the country club. After double-checking that my hair was orderly, I made my way into the club.

I had gotten used to this similar routine at other networking events. As usual, a group of friendly people were at the front desk with sticky name tags and colorful markers. Stating my legal, more professional-sounding name, I took a blue marker and wrote it down on a name tag and placed it on the left side of my chest.

Not knowing anybody, I went straight for the bar to grab a cocktail to hold in my hand. The line was reasonably long, so I struck up a conversation with the gentleman in front of me, who told me that this was not his first event. Feeling somewhat relieved to have found someone who knew his lay of the land, I told him my educational background and motivation for attending. Without divulging in detail about my living situation, I dodged some uncomfortable questions by keeping things vague. I was afraid that if he knew about who I was staying with and any other details in that realm, I would be looked down upon and not taken seriously.

The gentleman in front of me bought me a cocktail at the bar and offered to introduce me to his group of friends. The group, as was customary in Palm Springs, was comprised of middle-aged gay men of various professional backgrounds.

As a newcomer, I basked for a few minutes being the center of attention of the group. They all asked me questions about my background, educational and personal, and my professional aspirations. I indicated that I was looking for a job in the area, working on the campaign, or something involving public policy. Several of the men knew about the campaign but were not directly affiliated with it, nor were they connected to local politics. They suggested to me that this time, however, the candidate I had shown interest in working for had a better shot at winning this time around.

*Sweet! These guys are locals, and they feel good about the candidate. Maybe, if I can get a job on the campaign, it will translate to getting a job with the candidate in D.C. after the election is over! I can finally put my hard work to good use. This feels like the silver lining I had been looking for!*

After feeling confident for a few minutes, my intuition started to sense that something was off. I couldn't quite pinpoint it, but something in the pit of my stomach was telling my brain that there was something wrong here. When I would ask the gentleman in the group if they knew anyone who worked for the campaign, the conversation would then immediately shift to them talking about a certain individual who was affiliated, and that I should meet this person at a pool party.

*A pool party? That sounds like fun, but that seems like a very odd place to do business, right? Like, I understand things are different down here, and I'm in no position to judge, but this is weird, right? Like, hello, I want to work on the campaign, here's my speedo. Weird?*

After a while, I began analyzing the faces and body language of some other attendees. Suddenly, I began to realize why I was feeling so unsettled. It did not at all feel like anyone was interested in my resume. At all. People were looking at me, not like they wanted to hire me, but like they wanted to sleep with me. I began to feel very uneasy and even slightly paranoid. My mind reverted to the negative line of thinking that this little life reset was supposed to fix.

*Calm down. They just like what they see, that's all. Don't worry, keep cool. No! Fuck that! How many people here are looking at me because they want to hire me? And if they do want to hire me, is it going to be a job where I use my fucking brain or am I just going to be a prop for rich dudes at social functions down here? Hey, quit complaining; things could be a lot worse. You could be back at home having all of these shitty thoughts, right? Sure, same shitty thoughts, different location. How marvelous. They just want to help, stop freaking yourself out. A lot of these guys seem nice! I don't care, something doesn't feel right.*

This feeling did not shake. I had hoped that it was all in my head, but the longer I stayed at the mixer, the more uncomfortable I felt. There was no escaping this feeling. The only two times when I felt like I got any attention paid to me in the last year were go-go dancing and whatever the hell I was doing in Palm Springs; both were due to how I looked and nothing else. Even when I tried to redirect the conversation to my academic background, language skills, or career prospects, I could tell that eyes and attention were clearly drifting elsewhere. This felt like a sign.

I'd had enough.

I left the country club as quickly as I could and raced my crappy car back to my host's house. After scurrying quickly down the steps, I rummaged about for the sexiest outfit I could find.

*Relax. It's been a long day, you need to sleep. No, seize the day and sleep later! Ok, chill. Maybe you should lie down for a bit? No, fuck that. I'm sexy now—time to get my money's worth.*

After throwing the outfit on underneath my clothes, I got back in the car and bolted over to the Arenas neighborhood of Palm Springs, where all the gay bars were. My adrenaline was running high from this unshakeable feeling that no one would ever hire me for my brain.

*You know what? Fuck my brain! Who cares that I knew the difference between neoliberalism and neoconservatism? Who cares that I could deliver lectures on globalization, political philosophy, or economic development? Who cares that I could read and write in traditional and simplified Chinese characters? Nobody seems to care. My body was the only thing getting me any shred of attention. Time to cash the fuck in.*

I parked my car in front of the first bar I could find. Assassins, a bar on the corner of the Arenas district, was my first stop. It was still relatively early in the evening, but because Daylight Saving had not begun, the sky outside was becoming very dark. I walked in with the most straight-up confidence. I even considered just hopping onto a box and dancing until someone stopped me, on the off chance that the bet would pay off. I was confident, but not stupid.

The first bartender I could find seemed a little alarmed by how quickly and aggressively I approached him.

"Where is your manager, sir?" I asked forcefully.

"Um, I'm the manager," the man in front of me said, still a little bit startled by my abrasive entrance.

"Oh. Well, hello there. My name is DJ, and I want to dance here," I said, grabbing his hand and shaking it firmly.

"You, you want to dance here?" the man asked, still very confused.

"Yes. I live here now. And I would like to dance. I have go-go danced before, and I would like to do it again here," I said, loudly and confidently.

The man, whose name I still did not know, paused for a moment. He had clearly processed my rather dramatic entrance and then proceeded to check me out, his eyes making their way up and down my frame.

"I see. Ok, well, my name is Larry," he said.

"Nice to meet you, Larry," I said, through my teeth with a forced smile.

"You said you've go-go danced before, is that correct?" he asked.

"Yes, this won't be my first rodeo," I said, even though it would only be my second.

"Show me your abs," Larry said.

Without even skipping a beat, I flexed my abdominal muscles, lifted my shirt, and showed him my abs.

"Yeah, you're good," Larry said. "Are you free right now?"

*Wait, what the what? Did he just say now? He said now, oh my god, he said right now as in right fucking now!*

My stomach dropped, and my heart began racing. I had just hoped to get an audition some other time, but now I was asked to dance on the spot. Holy crap.

"Um, I mean sure," I said. The confidence I had walked in with had been thrown off by an offer out of left field. "Yes, I am absolutely free now. In fact, I am free all night."

"Wow, very committed! We love to hear that. Do you have a jock or a thong with you?" Larry asked.

"Yes, I'm wearing one right now," I said, lowering my pants so that he could see the waistband of my jockstrap.

"That'll do. See those swinging doors over there? You're going to want to go through them and ask for Curtis; he'll take you to the dressing room. Put your stuff in one of the little cubbies and get ready.

There is oil in there to make your skin look nice and shiny, and knee pads if you need them. Some of our dancers like to twerk on their knees," Larry said.

He then laughed an awkward laugh that reminded me of a hyena, kind of loud and shrill. I tried to hide my reaction as best I could. I was in absolutely no position to bite the hand that was about to feed me. Hyena laugh notwithstanding, I was grateful to have gotten this opportunity and lucky that it had happened so quickly.

"Once you are undressed and ready, come back out here and dance on any empty box you see. We'll have you on for half an hour and see how you do. Keep all the tips you make, and we'll talk afterwards. Sound good?" Larry asked, giving a more subtle version of his awkward laughter.

"Sounds good," I said.

"Would you like a shot?" he asked.

"Sure. Hit me," I said.

Larry pulled out the handle and gestured for me to lean back so he could pour the alcohol directly into my mouth.

*Fuck, it's the devil's piss. Gross. Whatever. I'll be a tequila lover if that means I can get booked.*

Well. That was fast. Confidence, determination, and maybe a little positivity did go a long way. I found Curtis, who proceeded to lead me to the dressing room, where I quickly stripped down to my jock-strap and rubbed the oil all over my body, perhaps a little too liberally.

"Ok, so we'll have you on box one, that's right across from the bar, it's the only one that doesn't have a dancer now. Give it your best shot, cutie," Curtis said, winking at me.

I strutted confidently out of the dressing room giving absolutely no fucks at all. Hopping onto the empty box, I started dancing like rent was due. I flipped my hair back and forth, trying to attract attention. Before long, a few gentlemen over at the bar started looking at me. It started with just one or two, then the whole table was looking over. Since I had my audience, I turned up the charm even more. I spun around and tried to make sure they got a full 360-degree view. Unlike my dance audition at the showcase, these guys were looking at me for the *right* reasons.

All of a sudden, a completely separate pair of guys came over to tip me.

*Oh my god, is that $20? Holy shit. Keep going; if people see that you're getting tipped twenty-dollar bills, that'll make others want to tip that high. Now start thrusting, slut! Yes! You're doing it! Keep going!*

The gentlemen who tipped me went back to their table, and *another* group of guys came over this time with wads of ten-dollar bills. They had me turn so that they could fit Mr. Hamilton in every single part of my Andrew Christian jockstrap, including the straps that held my cheeks.

Finally, a couple of guys from the group of gentlemen who had been watching me came over. They had their hands behind their backs and looked up at me on the box, just observing. I turned the charm on to the maximum level. I ran my fingers through my hair and rolled my eyes to the back of my head as though I was experiencing the best orgasm of my life. I tilted my head back down to wink at them.

*Oh. My. God. That's..... that's...*

Both gentlemen reached behind their backs and pulled out hundred-dollar bills in each of their hands. Each. Each!

*$400? Holy crap! Bring on the Benjamins!*

My heart was racing faster than it ever had. I started to slow down out of fear that I would have a heart attack. I started grinding as I winked at the two gentlemen. They winked back, reached into their pockets, and pulled out *another* pair of hundred-dollar bills.

*What the hell? How is this even happening? Is this all I had to do? Why didn't I come dance here instead of Fresno? Hell, why didn't I come here instead of going to college? Who cares about brainpower? I've made more money now in the first ten minutes here than I have in years.*

As I kept dancing harder and faster, trying not to keep the mountains of bills piling up in my underwear, another group of guys stood behind the gentlemen with the hundred-dollar bills.

*A line? Is that a line? I have a line of guys wanting to tip me. This is insane!*

Then another group of guys followed, and I could see out of the corner of my eye that Curtis and Larry were both taking notice, seeing that I could bring in a crowd and work it. This had to be nothing but good news. I was so excited that I could hardly contain myself. This was the best night ever!

I turned around and let out a loud shriek of euphoria. I threw my head back and looked up at the ceiling, smiling from ear to ear. I couldn't have asked for a better night, everything had been so spontaneous and yet so organic! I was on cloud nine.

But suddenly, that same awkward feeling from the networking event hit me square in the gut. Something began to feel off, even though I couldn't quite explain it. The feeling started when I began to feel a prickly pain developing in my underwear. The wads of dollar bills piling up in my jockstrap produced a poking sensation that was beginning to feel very uncomfortable. I reached down to try and organize the bills so that they wouldn't prick into my skin, but immediately felt a worse, sharper pain coming from the bills. I looked down into my waistband and did not see wads of dollar bills but rather a single rose.

*Um, who the hell put a rose into my waistband?*

Soon, I began to notice that it wasn't just one rose but two or three. As I pulled my waistband out, I noticed that there were more rose stems than dollar bills.

*What the hell is this?*

Trying to relieve myself of the pain, I gritted my teeth and tried pulling one of the roses out of my jockstrap, causing my right index finger to bleed. As soon as the rose came out, the petals immediately wilted off the stem and onto my go-go box, turning to ash. Dropping the thorny stem to the ground, I reached for another one, and it did the same thing. Ashes began accumulating below me and forming a dirt mound beneath my feet.

I started to hear a chorus of loud noises coming from the crowd behind me. Some of them were grunts, others were shrieks that began low but grew louder and creepier. I turned around to find that the crowd of men had all morphed into animals. Looking from left to right, the colors of the bar had all shone down to reveal a different colored animal. Pink rhinoceroses grunted in the back of the bar, yellow elephants trumpeted on either side of them, while royal blue monkeys swung from vines that had appeared above me from out of nowhere.

*What the hell is going on? Am I tripping? What was in that tequila shot I took when I got here?*

The ashes began to sink the box further and further into the ground. I looked beneath me and saw yellow, orange, and blue snakes slithering around the box.

*I am definitely tripping right now. What the hell is going on? Did Larry put something in my drink? This is why I never drink the devil's piss!*

Not wanting to get closer to the snakes, I jumped as high as I could off the box and, to my surprise, began floating high in the air. I had no idea where to go; I wanted to avoid the aggressive animals on the ground, but didn't want to hit the monkeys or the vines. Not knowing how to control myself, my eyes caught the bathroom sign, and I immediately soared over.

After managing to float my way to the sink, I immediately looked into the mirror.

*What the actual fuck? Is that me? Is that- am I a toucan?*

Staring deeply into the mirror, I did not see a human being looking back at me. I saw a black toucan with an extremely colorful beak lined with lime green, ruby red, and bright purple. I tried my best to look myself in the eyes, but I couldn't, they were too small and beady. Not to mention that my beak kept getting in the way.

*This isn't happening. This is not happening. I've gone through a lot of crazy shit in the past year but this is fucking weird. I'm not an exotic animal, I'm a human being, goddammit!*

Just as I thought things weren't going to get weirder, I could see through the reflection behind me that the stall door was opening slowly and eerily. Atop a bright green zebra with purple stripes sat a band of multicolored neon baboons growling their teeth at me menacingly. They looked at me like they wanted to kill me. As soon as one of them snapped its teeth at me, I flew as high as I could out of the bathroom.

The bar had become a zoo, a safari, and a circus all in one. Animals from every realm of the animal kingdom in every shade roared, squawked, and howled at the top of their lungs. I flapped my wings as hard as I could, attempting to remain above the chaos. Flapping harder and harder, it became increasingly difficult to breathe. Looking over at the bar for help, I did not see Larry or Curtis but rather two cackling red and blue hyenas ravenously circling the bar. Just when my heart was about ready to give out, I looked beneath me and a bright blue jaguar jumped up at me, its mouth wide open.

Then, I woke up from my nap; the bizarre nightmare I'd been having had ended.

After I returned from the mixer, I must have conked out immediately. I'm not sure how long I had been sleeping, but judging from the fact that it was still light outside, it was probably not very long. I sat up in bed, massaged my forehead, and looked over at my suit jacket lying on the floor beneath me. It still had my nametag sticker on it from the work event earlier that afternoon and was full of "business cards" and not multiple hundred-dollar bills.

The sheets I was sleeping on had just been washed and pressed by the housekeepers, and the crisp cleanliness of the sheets felt great against my bare skin. I sat there for almost another hour just tossing and turning, not wanting to get out of bed.

Finally, I felt hungry enough to go up and make myself a smoothie. I walked upstairs and made my way past the tall glass windows to the kitchen. I pressed the automatic awning, and the curtains revealed one of those perfect evenings. The temperature sat at a pleasant, warm 72 degrees. Every single color I could see around me was much more heightened than normal. The blue sky was bluer, the snowcapped mountains were the palest shade of white, the grassy green golf course was greener than usual, and the pool umbrellas lingering over the lounge chairs beamed a bright shade of firehouse red.

I blended myself my favorite wild-berry fruit smoothie as I looked over at all the colors awaiting me outside. After my smoothie was finished blending, I put on my sunglasses and opened the large glass doors that led to the pool area. The jets were already swirling the turquoise blue water in the jacuzzi. I placed the smoothie on the table next to my lounge chair and dove into the pool headfirst. On such a perfectly sunny day, the pool water stood at a perfect temperature. I emerged on the other side of the pool and felt like I was in a freaking cologne commercial. Even though the weather was perfect, it still felt a little chilly getting out of the pool, so I decided to dunk in the jacuzzi before lying out for a full-body tan. The jacuzzi water almost instantly warmed every inch of my cold skin; I could feel it swiftly smoothing out my goosebumps one by one. I looked up at the mountains and took several deep breaths, trying to enjoy every second of my time alone.

When I began to feel a tad pruned, I got out of the hot tub and made my way over to my chair. I relaxed myself down on my back and felt the drips of water melt down my body like a popsicle on a hot summer's day, only this weather was not sweltering hot; it was a perfect spring day outside.

Uncomfortable with the silence, I connected my phone to the surround sound system in the house and found a playlist with nothing but calm, soothing music. I closed my eyes for a few minutes to soak in every bit of this seemingly perfect backdrop. I relaxed for a few minutes on the lounge chair, sipping my smoothie and listening to the calming music.

And then it hit me: I was still not happy.

Every bit about this day, on paper, was perfect. The location. The weather. The scenery. The music. The ambience. Outside, everything was perfectly marvelous. Inside, I still felt incredibly empty.

I pulled out my phone and started texting people. Since Damien bartended at night, I called him during the day. The call went immediately to voicemail. He sent me an automatic text saying that he was busy and couldn't talk. So, I started calling Gavin, who had a similar crazy work schedule. That call also went to voicemail.

Then, I started calling a few of my cousins. Since we all lived in different time zones, there was always at least one cousin who would pick up the phone when I was having a moment. Not this time.

*Chill out. People are just busy during the day, it's not like they're intentionally ignoring you. Calm down. No, fuck you. How about you don't calm down? They are doing this on purpose because you're too much to handle. Go to the bar refrigerator and find one of your more reliable friends.*

Out of frustration, I threw my phone onto the other lounge chair and looked up at the bright blue sky above me. Not a single cloud blemished that perfect blue canvas. I watched as birds chased each other back and forth before darting back into the trees. At that particular moment, I was jealous of them. Cliché as it sounds, I felt like I was a bird in a gilded cage. Extreme luxury and comfort couldn't free me from the aching feeling of complete solitude. After a few minutes, my phone rang. I had assumed it was one of the people whom I had called. It was not. The call was from Michelle.

I hesitated even taking the call and nearly let it go to voicemail. While we had not had a falling out per se, I did not like the way that our last conversation ended.

"Hello?" I asked.

"Hey, Uncle DJ," Michelle said softly.

For a few seconds, I paused. I had no idea what she was talking about for a good seven seconds. And then it hit me.

"When?" I asked.

"About half an hour ago," she said.

"Boy or girl?" I asked.

"Girl. Mom and baby are both healthy and doing fine," she said.

This was spectacular news, but I had no idea what to say next. One of my very closest friends had just given birth to her very first child. A child that, mind you, she and Brad had been waiting a very long time to have. All those years of heartache and patience had paid off. Now, she was a mother, and Brad was a father. I couldn't process everything.

"I—that's…" I struggled to find the words to say.

The shock from the news had still not worn off. The music continued to play in the background as I attempted to find the words to say.

*Apologize for making your friends worried sick, you psycho. No, say congrat-ulations on the baby! What, to the sister? The sister didn't push out the kid; why would you congratulate her? This silence is fucking awkward. Say something!*

Right before I could even say anything, Michelle chimed in.

"We miss you, DJ. A lot. And your niece can't wait to meet her Uncle DJ as soon as you're ready," she said graciously.

I paused for a little while longer, hoping that I wouldn't put my foot in my mouth or say something to make the situation even more awkward.

"Well, um, I'm excited to meet her too," I said. "Thanks for calling. Please give my best to Lauren."

"I will. Hope to hear from you soon," she said.

The phone call ended, and I stared at the reflection of the water on the bottom of the pool. My eyes followed the little inflatable mattress floating aimlessly alone across the pool. I tried to stabilize and start to feel something, anything. Something miraculous had just happened; why the hell wasn't I feeling anything?

*It's all the gallons of liquor you've been drinking, shithead. Ok, I have not been drinking gallons. Shush. And that can't be the only reason, right? Well, it's not helping. Is the drinking making the depression worse, or is the depression making me drink worse? How does one even answer that question?*

I walked up to the edge of the pool and faced downward. In another part of the state, my best friend was holding a newborn baby girl she had longed for while the rest of my friends rallied to celebrate. And I was here, alone in a massive luxury home, dreaming about dancing for random strangers and somehow unable to feel any kind of emotional reaction to the news. Attempting to feel *something*, I fell face down into the pool and did a belly flop.

My stomach hurt like hell when I got out of the water, so mission accomplished, I guess. Even though it was painful, at least I felt some-thing. I got out of the pool and went back to the lounge chair. I returned to lying on my back and put my sunglasses on, wanting to soak in the rest of this beautiful day as much as I could while my stomach recovered from the belly flop.

It was a very overwhelming feeling, but I truly did not feel any more or less depressed there than I did when I was living back at home with my family. Truth be told, I would much rather be depressed and lonely in a nice ass home in Palm Springs but I was beginning to feel stuck.

*This isn't working, I'm still sad. Well, of course, you're still sad; you're drinking a ton and not working. Way to go, Einstein.*

Since I was not making any progress professionally, felt like I was falling further into lethargy, and was away from the people that I cared about, I decided to leave Palm Springs. Paradise was pleasant, but by the time I departed, I felt like it was all just one big beautiful mirage.

# CHAPTER 5

## THE EMERALD CITY

After I returned home from Palm Springs, it was time to go back to the drawing board. My time in the desert did hardly anything for me professionally and, counterintuitively, worsened my self-esteem. I did get to see some cool performances, visit some nice places, and enjoy a change of scenery. But April was fast approaching, and I began to fear that I would make it to a full year without having a job. It was time to change course, again.

One place I had kept returning to was the careers section of my university's alumni page. I had applied for multiple jobs there and, shocker, never heard back from the vast majority of them. Something about that stupid online firewall was preventing me from even getting a response from a human being. Since a solid majority of the jobs to which I applied were in New York City and Washington, D.C., it became clear to me that I needed to break through that frustratingly dense jobs portal firewall. In addition, my little getaway to Palm Springs had shown me that I needed to be seen as a serious professional and not just as some brainless ingenue with nothing to offer but my fit tummy.

With generous assistance from my parents, again, I booked a round-trip ticket for the East Coast. I would fly into New York for a few days, commute by train for a few days in D.C., and then head home. One week, I thought, again very naively, was enough to hand in my resume in person to a variety of organizations that had been ignoring my online applications and pestering emails. I figured if employers were to see how eager and willing I was to work by flying several thousand miles to the other side of the country, then they would be more willing to give my application another look. Yes, I was that naïve.

As much as I love my West Coast and will always defend it as the best coast, I absolutely love visiting D.C. and New York City. Situated some 3,000 miles away from my beloved Golden State are two cities that offer so much for a person obsessed with both history and musical theater. Over a decade earlier, I had saved up my allowance and lawn mowing money for a school-sponsored trip to visit both cities during the summer between junior high and high school. I still remember each moment so vividly: my first walk through the National Mall, my first time seeing the White House, my first stroll through Times Square, and my first Broadway show. The trip was practically perfect.

The trip I would embark upon in the spring of 2023 would be yet another iteration of the serotonin exodus with a firm, bitter dose of reality. This time, I would not be venturing out east as a dewy-eyed 14-year-old with fantastical dreams of seeing the Lincoln Memorial or my first Broadway show; I would be going as a jaded, depressed 27-year-old desperate for *someone* to give my resume a longer look than the obstinate cybersphere had.

To cut down on travel costs, I planned to couch surf with my cousin Kiana in D.C. and my friend Diego in New York. A fellow theater friend, Diego, and I had met doing community theater together in the Central Valley. While we differ in many different aspects, he was, and still is, another rare friend with whom I don't need to communicate verbally to feel understood. Just one look, and that's it.

The bus ride from Newark Airport to the train station in midtown Manhattan should have felt invigorating. On repeat, I played Taylor

Swift's anthem "Welcome to New York" and looked out at that big, beautiful skyline, longing for it to fill me with a sense of childlike wonderment and possibility. It did not.

When I finally got to Diego's apartment after navigating the convoluted New York City subway system, he opened the door and greeted me with a huge hug. I was trying my best to convey my gratitude, but also be authentic in how I felt.

After greeting his very affectionate boyfriend Gabriel and their even more affectionate doggo named Luna, I plopped myself onto the couch. Wine and pizza were on the coffee table waiting for me to eat and drink my shitty feelings away.

*Here we go. It really is the little things. God, this pizza is so delicious. I really hope that's not the only bottle of wine they have. Like, seriously.*

Both Diego and Gabriel had been checking in on me during my decline, so there wasn't very much to catch up on besides the uneventful flight from California and the uninspiring bus ride from New Jersey.

"Is it still bad?" Diego asked, looking deeply into my eyes.

"Yes," I said.

"How bad?" he asked.

"Still really fucking bad," I said, bluntly.

We looked into each other's eyes for several seconds. He understood my pain and didn't even need to ask follow-up questions. I fought back tears with limited success. Diego reached out and held my hand.

"You just want to sleep it off?" he asked.

"Yeah," I said.

Diego and Gabriel both gave me long hugs, prepared the couch for me to sleep on, and then went to bed. Unfortunately, the only blanket they had was a weighted blanket. When you're depressed or anxious, having more weight on you is usually not a good thing. I struggled to get comfortable on the couch.

*Way to go, homie. Now, you get to be a failure on a different coast. Whatever, maybe I'll win the lottery. Or maybe I'll get hit by a train, nothing surprises me at this point. Maybe you could be a street performer? Maybe you'll bump into a casting agent and get an audition. Yeah, like that'll happen. I could also get kidnapped and wake up without a kidney. Just go the fuck to sleep. That's a tomorrow problem.*

I woke up the next morning, not sure where I was. The living room where I was sleeping was nearly pitch black. Not knowing what time it was, I felt around for my phone. It was 12:45.

*Holy crap, that had better be AM.*

Nope. It was past noon. I guess my body was still on California time or depression time; probably a little of both. I played around on my phone for a little while, then fell back asleep for another few hours.

After waking up close to five, I realized I had pretty much slept the day away. A part of me was nervous about all the time I was wasting. However, I had gotten used to this feeling: when my body tells me it needs to rest, it needs to rest. Thankfully, I had another full couple of days to pass out the stack of resumes I brought with me.

When Gabriel returned from work, he immediately stripped down to his birthday suit.

Diego, who had been working in the room next door, came into the living room a few minutes later. He was fully naked, holding several different containers of lube.

"You boys ready to have some fun?" he asked us.

It was very difficult to get myself in the mood to have fun; my idea of fun at that moment was to just sit, sulk, and perhaps have some more alcohol. However, my therapist had mentioned to me that one of the many things I should do to boost my mood was more of, and I quote, the "M" word. It felt like going to the gym or eating super healthy: it wasn't my first choice, but I knew it was something that needed to be done to better myself.

*Your friends are trying to give you a hand. Let them.*

Once I said I was game, my pants quickly came off, and then my shirt. Once my underwear dropped to the ground, I leaned back on the couch and watched Diego play with Gabriel. While I wasn't completely limp, it was a challenge getting aroused in a situation that would normally make me go full mast instantly. It felt like I was eating a frozen pizza that had only been partially reheated. Some parts of that pizza are sizzling hot, others are still frozen, and some of it is somewhat in between.

After helping me edge for about an hour, I miraculously managed to have an orgasm. I had not had the energy or libido to climax very often, so this was a flooding of my swimmers in the reserves.

"I'll go get a towel. A big towel," Gabriel said, looking at my glazed torso in amazement and laughing at his little joke.

"Do you guys want to finish?" I asked Diego.

"No, we're good. We might finish later," he said.

"Are you sure? I can help get you both over the edge," I offered.

"It's ok, we're good for now. We might finish before we go to bed, but for now, I'm hungry," he insisted, pulling out his phone to order food.

Gabriel came back and helped me clean myself up.

"This is a lot. I think I'm going to need to shower," I said, laughing awkwardly.

"Go for it, we'll get your pasta ordered and see you when you get out," Diego said, pinching my left butt cheek.

"Good, send in the carbs," I laughed as I headed to the bathroom.

I showered slowly, lathering my skin with body wash in every direction. Reminded of my time in Palm Springs, where I belly-flopped trying to feel something, I paused and felt gratitude for having felt something again. When you're depressed, the experiences that normally give you pleasure or joy simply don't. You could be lying down in a luxurious backyard by a fantastic pool, witnessing the colors and vivacity of a beautiful city, or engaging in sexual activity with your homies, and still feel completely empty. While I was still not feeling myself, I felt grateful that I had friends around me to give me a helping hand, figuratively and literally.

Returning from the bathroom, I put my underwear on and enjoyed an evening filled with movies and pasta with Diego and Gabriel. Their dog Luna sat at our feet while we feasted on fettuccine and garlic bread. I felt slightly invigorated, a bit more confident, and well fed. Tomorrow was a new day about which I felt cautiously optimistic.

The next morning, I miraculously woke up a lot earlier than I thought I would, around eight. Good thing too, I had a whole stack of resumes to drop off and was ready to impress some employers with my tenacity and, hopefully, schedule some interviews. I showered and brushed my teeth, trying to polish off my gloomy demeanor as best I could. My outfit complemented my figure perfectly, and I was having a good hair day, much to my relief.

At about half past nine, I stepped into the living room to say goodbye to Gabriel and Diego, both of whom were lounging semi-naked while they worked from home.

"See you boys later, I'm off," I said.

"Damn, boy. Wait, a minute. Give us a little twirl," Diego said.

I rolled my eyes and did a 360 for them while they whistled.

"Hot damn, you look so debonair and sharp in that suit. Kick some ass, you sexy brainy beast!" Gabriel hollered, making me roll my eyes again.

"Ok, bye," I said.

"We'll meet you in Times Square around seven!" Diego shouted as I left. "Knock them dead!"

I headed for the subway and embarked on the trek down Manhattan. The first series of offices I went to were mainly downtown: a few campaign offices, some think tanks, and a bank. With each of them, I had trouble getting past the doorman or finding an office with someone willing to meet with me. I was either turned away, sent to the wrong location by my maps, given a business card with a phone number that sent me directly to voicemail, or told to apply online. The resumes I left either at the front desk or in the mailboxes probably went straight into the shredder after I left.

*Maybe this AI firewall isn't the only thing in my way. Maybe I'm just cursed.*

Frustrated but trying not to get too discouraged, I saved my ideal potential job for last. During graduate school, I had learned about a think tank in New York City that needed specialists who had a deep knowledge of Asian politics and proficiency in an Asian language. It was a non-profit, but the pay was good, and the organization appeared to have a solid reputation. In my view, it was a perfect fit for me, but the organization had never reached out to me. I applied many times on their online portal, sent them my resume via email countless times, and even tried reaching out to some of their board members on social media. Now that I was there in person, I was eager to show just how eager I was to work with them and finally get my resume seen by a human being.

Unfortunately, the address on their website had not been updated. All of my map applications on my phone sent me to wrong locations, as poetic as could be, on different sides of Manhattan. I ran to the financial district and learned that they had left that location over 10 years prior. I trained up to the Upper East Side and learned they had also moved locations. Running around Manhattan like a madman, I stopped at a coffee shop to take a break. Wiping the sweat off the corners of my face, I began breathing as my therapist had instructed.

*You're not on fire, the sky is not falling, it is a beautiful day in New York, and you're just lost. That's all.*

I tried calming myself down by sending funny memes to Damien, Gavin, and Enrique. None of them responded.

*It's fine. They're busy, they have jobs, they'll respond when they can. You're going to get a job today, and then they'll message you funny memes when you're at work! Think positive!*

Finally, after arriving at the final wrong location, I was able to ascertain the correct address from a polite doorman who wrote down the address on a piece of paper and handed it to me.

*Oh my god, are you kidding me?*

The office was located on 42nd Street and Broadway, how perfect! A non-profit where I could use my Chinese to help the world during the day, and then just clock out of work and go see a Broadway show after? For a theater kid with my academic background, this could not have been a more perfect intersection between my greatest interests.

Feeling like Dorothy when she entered the massive gates of the

Emerald City, I walked into the building with so much excitement and pride in myself. I worked very hard to get to where I was at that moment. Everything on my resume was completely genuine, and it lined up perfectly with this organization. Nevertheless, I tried to maintain my cool as best I could.

After walking into the building, I approached the doorman and we exchanged greetings.

"Hello there, I'm looking for this organization. Am I at the correct address?" I asked.

The receptionist looked at my phone very skeptically, with his brow raised.

"Yeah, this is the right place. Do you have an appointment?" he asked, looking somewhat annoyed.

*No, sir, I don't have a fucking appointment. That's why I'm here; nobody is responding to my emails! Ok, chill. He doesn't know all that; try and turn on the charm.*

"No, actually, I don't. But I really want to work here, I brought my resume and I'm hoping to speak with someone in person and hope-fully schedule a job interview," I said earnestly.

"I see. Well, we aren't really allowed to send people up to any of the offices unless you've got an appointment. I'm sorry, chief," he said.

Losing my patience, I placed both of my hands on the table and leaned forward slightly. I needed to express how desperate I was without coming across as too threatening.

"Listen, boss, I know this is going to sound ridiculous, but I'm not even from around here; I'm actually from California. I've been out of work for almost a year, I have student loans to pay off, and nobody is responding to my online applications. I've tried emailing a thousand times, and nothing seems to be working, so I flew all the way out here to drop off my resume in person," I said while staring into his eyes. "If I could just speak to someone one-on-one and demonstrate my will-ingness to work here, I think I might have a shot. I know I'm a complete stranger you just met two minutes ago, and this seems way out of left field, but could you please just help me out here?" I pleaded.

The receptionist stared me down for a few moments until he realized by my stoic face that I meant business. While maintaining his gaze on me, he picked up the phone and started dialing. I won this round. He mumbled into the receiver for a moment before hanging up.

"Ok, chief, I got good news and bad news," he said.

*Just spit it out, for fuck's sake. This is stressing me out.*

"You can't go up, but they're going to send somebody down," he said, throwing his hands up. "That's the best I could do."

I felt relieved and appreciative; he truly did not hold the power to get me a job, but he did all he could, and that's all I could have asked for. I thanked him and waited for my chance to finally talk to a human being from what was arguably my dream organization.

I began polishing my appearance, fixing my hair, and reciting my elevator pitch. With much anticipation, I looked intently toward the elevators. I took several more deep breaths to calm the butterflies down. This was the moment I had been waiting for.

*You've got this. This is your moment. You've done the work, and now it's all going to pay off. Dream job. Dream location. You've got the bump and the set, time to spike.*

After about five agonizingly slow minutes, someone who I presumed was an intern emerged from the elevator. Headphones still in her ears and staring mindlessly down at her phone, I hoped to god that this was not the individual that the doorman had summoned. Unfortunately, it was. She approached me with the most dismissive attitude possible that was still technically semi-professional.

"Hey, are you the guy with the resume?" she asked, showing minimal interest.

*Seriously? "The guy with the resume?" I flew over 3,000 miles to get here because you shit heads have not answered any of my emails. What a bitch.*

"Yeah! My name is DJ. I lived in Asia for a few years, I speak Mandarin, and I have both a bachelor's and master's degree from two really good schools," I said, handing her my resume.

She took it with one hand and held it with a slightly limp wrist. To say that she was skimming it would be a very generous description.

"That's cool. Well, have you applied on our website or emailed us?" she asked, with the same uninterested gaze.

*Yes, I have emailed you fucking fuckers multiple times and that's why my ass flew out here from fucking California so you could see how determined I am to get a goddamn job here, you bitchy fucking fuck!*

"Yes, I have. I've applied through the online portal a couple of times and also sent my resume to the email address listed on your website. I'm actually from California, I flew out here to make sure I could talk to someone in person about how much I'd love to work here," I said, trying to mask my anger with an enthusiastic disposition.

She continued to pretend to be interested in reading my resume.

"Ok. Well, if you email us, then we'll be in touch. Thanks," she said as she put her headphones back in and headed for the elevator.

Before I continue, I hope I have already conveyed that I am not in any way a violent person. I get angry and frustrated a lot, but have never acted violently. I am so much of an empath that I can hardly even watch horror movies without cringing.

And yet, as the intern walked away, something inside of me snapped. I was filled with so much pent-up resentment and frustration from the previous months, and felt like I had nothing to lose. This condescending intern came to personify all of the rejection and frustration I had felt over the past several months. I had been angry at an invisible internet firewall blocking my job prospects, but now, I saw someone emanating that rejection. It was at this moment that I had my very first vivid homicidal thought.

As she walked toward the elevator, I had this crazy vision of following her from behind and grabbing her aggressively by the hair.

*I'm sorry, I don't think you understood me clearly. Let's see if this will get your bitch-ass to understand. How does this fucking feel, huh? Oh, I'm sorry, you don't like your face being smashed into the ground like this? Well, you know what? I don't give a flying fuck. I'm so fucking done with this bullshit. Fuck you, you snide fucking bitch. I'm going to smash those goddamn fucking headphones into the fucking wall. Eat shit, bitch. Oh, I'm sorry, you think this is painful? That's too goddamn bad, I'm in fucking pain too and nobody, including and espe-*

*cially you, seems to understand or give a shit, so let me show you how pain feels, ugly cunt. Scream all you want, they're going to have to fucking shoot or taze me to get me to stop smashing your snide, ugly fucking face into the goddamn ground. I fucking hate you! I hope you fucking die! I hope your hideous soul burns in hell for all eternity, fucking bitch! Die! Die! Die!*

Obviously, I did not do or say any of that. I just stood there completely frozen. After my severe anger and homicidal thoughts reached a boiling point, my chin began to quiver after the intern had ascended, metaphorically and physically, back up to the office. The doorman, who had been watching, was speechless.

Now I knew how Dorothy felt when she left the Emerald City. It was not a grand magical city, it was just some lazy, phony shmuck behind a curtain. That curtain had now been lifted and, unlike Dorothy, I didn't have any goddamn slippers to carry me home.

I walked away from the magical land of Oz, tears slowly falling down my face, feeling defeated. My mind began to wander as I walked out into Times Square, my supposed happy place. Immediately, the previous ten years of my life flashed back in my head again. The particular moments flashing before my eyes were of late nights in Taipei, studying character after character after character and being frustrated that it would take hours just to be able to write a couple of simple sentences. Or holidays spent feeling depressed in my apartment alone, watching my social media feed display countless photos of friends and family enjoying seasonal merriment while I had to watch from abroad. Or spending hours upon hours on problem sets in grad school that would legitimately consume three hours of my life to complete one problem. To be clear, not one full homework assignment, but one problem.

The moment in the lobby was so surreal. I didn't feel like it had happened. Even though my boiling rage had subsided, the negative thoughts came back with a vengeance as I walked away from the building. I made myself even angrier and sadder.

*What in the actual fuck was that all for? Did I really intentionally put myself through intellectual and emotional hell for an entire decade for whatever that little encounter was? What a fucking bitch, I hope she gets hit by the goddamn subway. They're always pushing people in front of subways these days, I hope the next time I see this bitch, it's on the six o'clock news. Ok, she might have been having a bad day, so calm down. A bad day? A bad day? No, fuck that bitch. No, calm down. This is not who you were raised to be. You're better than this. Your parents raised you to be better than this, your friends know that you're better than this. Just calm down. Calm down? Why would I want to calm down? Who gives a fuck? I'm a fucking monster now, this is what monsters do.*

Distressed and defeated, I sat on the famous red stairs in the middle of Times Square, feeling like I was at the end of the line. I knew that this was just one organization in one city in one field, but this just seemed like the ultimate culmination of several months of non-stop rejection. I finally found my dream job in one of the greatest cities in the world, doing something I love, working for a non-profit, using my language skills and education, and in the most iconic of locations. And all I got was *that*.

After what felt like a lifetime of sitting on the stairs, stewing in my disillusioned thoughts, I managed to pick myself up and go for a walk around the theater district. I love looking at Broadway theaters, even from outside; it's one of my favorite things to do in that part of Manhattan.

While strolling through 47th Street, I saw a group of high school students cheerfully exit a school bus on what I assumed was a field trip to see a musical. Ironically, the theater they were walking into was playing *Hadestown*, a musical about hell. They all seemed very excited to be there, and my mood immediately shifted from depressed to a sense of melancholy. I used to be that happy and carefree because I thought I was bound to go somewhere in life. I wondered maybe when I was that age if someone else equally jaded had looked upon me and my friends with this same level of pensiveness.

The sun went down, and the lights in Times Square began to brighten. Diego and Gabriel got off work and met me for a burger. As soon as we sat down at the table, they wanted to hear an update on how my day went.

"So, how did today go? Did you get any good leads?" Diego asked.

I responded with a single facial expression.

"That bad, huh?" Diego asked.

I responded with my eyes; that's all it took.

"Well, I am really happy you came out to visit. Regardless of whether it is successful or not, we have loved having you here. We really missed you," Diego said.

*Yeah, but being a nice guy and being fun to be around is not a career opportunity. I need money, not friends, right now. And just, I don't know, some sense that the last fucking decade was not a complete waste of goddamn time.*

"I missed you boys too, a lot," I said, trying to be genuine but apparently unable to conceal my disappointment at how the day went.

"You know what? I have an idea," Gabriel said.

Within a flash, we were at a club in the West Village getting ready to watch a drag show. Gracious hosts that they were, they bought two rounds of shots and got me feeling pretty buzzed from the get-go. I was under the impression that this was going to be a very brief drag show and that we would just be enjoying a slow, quiet evening in the club. I'll blame my mood for that ridiculous expectation, as there is no such thing as a quiet evening at a gay club, particularly when there is a drag show.

Both Gabriel and Diego knew the main hostess, a drag queen named Sasha. After introducing the two of us, I noticed Gabriel whispering something into her ear. I didn't think anything of it, that is, until the show started.

"Ok, honeys! Welcome, welcome! It's pageant time! Let's see, I'm going to need three super sexy volunteers from the crowd," Sasha said loudly into the microphone.

"Right here!" both Diego and Gabriel shouted while shoving me towards the stage.

I was caught completely off guard. Normally, I am always the first to volunteer, particularly when there is performing involved. This time, however, I was barely ok with being out. I wanted so badly just to be back at the apartment in the dark, drinking wine and lying on the sofa. I'd have even settled for another round of our circle jerk but those two jackasses had other plans in mind.

Once I was on the stage, the lights made it hard to see into the audience. I could hear a lot of applause, whooping, and hollering. As had been the pattern for several months, I jumped into uncharted waters with little idea of what to do.

*Please tell me this isn't going to be a dance contest. Or a twerking competition. Or...I don't know; I just really hope whatever I've been volunteered for ends quickly.*

"Alright, thank you so much to our three sexy volunteers for volunteering for our little pageant," Sasha said.

My eyes had adjusted to the brightness in enough time to shoot a passive-aggressive scowl at Diego and Gabriel, who were howling with laughter in the audience.

"We're going to have three portions of the pageant. Each of you fabulous contestants will get a chance to show what you've got, and then we will choose the winner by applause. Does that sound good, everyone?" Sasha yelled emphatically.

*No. No, it does not.*

I forget exactly what the first two portions of the contest were, but I *definitely* remember what the last one was. We were told that the "talent" portion of the competition would be a contest to see who could imitate the most erotic orgasm.

*I am totally going to murder Diego and Gabriel in their sleep and make it look like an accident.*

"Alright, contestant number one: let's hear you squeal, honey," Sasha said.

Contestant number one was probably the most wasted out of the three of us. He just made a lot of noise and moaned really loudly. My head was right by the speaker, so I didn't care for contestant number one.

"Fabulous work, contestant number one! Very sexy. Contestant number two, show us what you got, baby," Sasha said.

Contestant number two was more sober and a little more subtle with his approach. He started out moaning softly and then built up to a very loud orgasm.

*Crap. You're next. I can barely get to an actual orgasm. How am I supposed to simulate one on stage? This is one skill that musical theater did not prepare me for.*

"And finally, we have contestant number three, give it your best shot," Sasha said, handing over the microphone to me.

I grabbed the microphone with the least amount of enthusiasm possible. By that point, thankfully, I was feeling the buzz from the shots earlier. I had no idea what else to do, so I defaulted to being funny. I paused momentarily, put my lips as close to the mic as possible, and dropped my voice as low as I could.

"You don't cum until daddy says you can cum," I bellowed from the base of my belly.

The audience lost it.

I could hear shrieking, clapping, fingers snapping, fans flapping, and howls of laughter coming from the crowd. Mission accomplished.

"Well. My God. That's the show. Thank you, everyone. Good night," Sasha said while seductively pretending to take me offstage.

As furious as I had been earlier that afternoon, I started to loosen up a bit. I even smiled a genuine little smile. The shots helped, to be sure, but being able to make people laugh again, be on a stage, and enjoy a night out with friends was definitely what my soul needed at that moment.

*Ok, fine. Diego and Gabriel get to live. I really hate it when my friends are right.*

My friends had gotten me to the point of smiling a genuine smile with the help of a friendly drag queen. The bar we were at was situated not too far from Stonewall. It reminded me that drag queens always have been and always will be the bedrock of our community. I was very appreciative to have been introduced to Sasha.

"Now that my lady parts have dried up from the talent portion, I think it's time that we choose the winner," Sasha said. "Remember, babes, you will applaud and scream for your candidate, and whoever gets the loudest applause is the winner! So, without further ado, will it be contestant number one?"

The group of contestant number one's friends, who were on his level, was a small but mighty force. They were the only ones applauding him, but they were quite loud.

"Ok, very nice, very nice. Now, contestant number two," Sasha said, placing her hand over his head.

Modest applause was given out for contestant number two, some cheers, and a catcall.

"Ok, and finally, we have contestant number three," Sasha said.

The audience roared with applause. Diego and Gabriel were by far the loudest, clapping and cheering at the top of their lungs. This made me feel slightly emotional. It felt nice to feel the kind of love and support that I had not felt while languishing by myself over the past few months.

My prize, an extra two shots from the bar, were served on a little platter by Sasha offstage. I downed both of them without a chaser and gave the tiny glasses back to her as she stared at me in disbelief.

"I went to a party school; chasers are for weenies," I joked, with a little wink to Sasha.

"So, your friends told me you're a go-go dancer," she said.

"Well, my friends were being very generous with that description. I did it once back in my hometown as a sort of trial run, but they didn't book me again after that," I said.

"Well, it's probably because you were the only twink at a bear event," she said.

*What the fuck, Diego and Gabriel? How much did you guys tell her? Does she have my address and social security number, too?*

"I mean that's part of it, but I'm also not a great dancer," I said meekly.

"Look at me, babe," she said.

I acquiesced.

"I see a lot of boys up on this stage every week: go-go boys, strippers, open mic attendees, and pageant contestants like tonight. You have something, you've got a quiet charisma that is very attractive. If you found a bar that hosted something other than a bear night, you could definitely get booked."

*Well, that's not exactly the kind of job I flew out here to get, but a paycheck is a paycheck, I guess.*

I looked back into Sasha's eyes and could tell that she meant what she said. We may or may not have made out a little before Diego and Gabriel dragged me home.


I was glad the trip ended on a happy note because panic began the next morning when I arrived at the train station to head south for the capital. All the resumes I had handed out were probably in the dumpster by now.

*Did you get a job? Did you do anything on this trip besides get rejected multiple places, jerk off with your friends, and go clubbing? You're going back home now without a job, again. Loser. Fucking loser. You have now been to how many cities, and you are still not able to get a job? How many more cities is it finally going to take for someone to hire you? You should probably give up. That snarky intern has a job and you don't, maybe you should be a bitch.*

To drown out the barrage of negative and anxiety-inducing thoughts, I started blasting rap music into my ears, which I hardly ever do. I probably should have picked something more soothing, like classical music, but I was not at all in the mood to feel comforted. I wished I could have just basked in the brief moments of happiness and community I felt at the bar, but as reality hit, all I could do was stew in the rage.

The train ride to D.C. was uneventful. I felt numb again, not feeling that this trip would be any different. Unfortunately, that feeling was correct. Every single person I talked to told me I needed to apply online, or looked at me like I was a crazy person for going in person. Based on my horrendous and detailed vision back in New York, I can't say that I blamed them for thinking that.

At the very least, I spent some quality time with my cousin Kiana and her fiancé Adam. Eager to change the subject from my job search, we talked about their upcoming wedding in Colorado later in the summer. They were both concerned about my professional and mental state, but, like Gabriel and Diego, did all they could to cheer me up.

We visited the National Mall, went out for drinks, and had a tipsy dance party in the living room. I tried my best to put on a happy face, but the lingering disappointment made it more difficult to fake it.

The trip overall had been very disheartening. If I didn't hear back from employers when I applied online and I got the door slammed in my face when I went in person, how the fuck was I supposed to find a job?

Flying back to California, these questions did not leave my mind as much as angsty Eminem, and a little dash of Pink, tried to help me cope with them. It seemed like there was no end in sight for anything job-related. I ended up back home and back at square one.

# Chapter 6

# Un Tope Grande en la Calle

A few days after my unsuccessful experiences on the East Coast and Palm Springs, I received a phone call from my very good friend Charles, whom I had met in language school in Mexico a few years before. Born in Hong Kong when it was still occupied by the British, Charles was trilingual before he was even in kindergarten (English, Cantonese, and Mandarin) and continued learning languages throughout his life. He claims that he can speak nine languages, but frankly, I think he's being modest. That number is probably closer to 12 or 13. Did I mention he's my age?

Two of the languages that Charles can speak are indigenous languages from Mexico. One of his many passions includes going to different sites and filming himself utilizing his language skills. He is absolutely brilliant, but also very shy and isn't always comfortable asking random strangers to film him. When he called me to share that he was preparing to do a nine-day journey of the Yucatán Peninsula, he offered to buy my plane ticket if I would cover a few of our meals in exchange for helping him navigate the terrain and film him. I had nothing to lose, really; it wasn't like I was holding out on some big opportunity. I knew that I just needed to not be alone and, preferably, around people who cared about me.

When I landed in Mexico, I was greeted by Charles at baggage claim. Just like Diego and Gabriel, he had been following my emotional descent via social media, so he greeted me with more warmth and enthusiasm than normal. We headed out of the airport and hailed a cab.

We ended up at a restaurant on the side of Mexico City where all the major nightclubs happened to be. Out of character, Charles suggested that we go out for a couple of drinks at some of the clubs before we headed back home. I declined; my travel day had already been long, and we had another long travel day ahead of us. Charles, the introvert, wanting to take me, the extrovert, out for the evening seemed just as weird as me, the extrovert, declining.

Still, we had to pass by the bars on our way back to Charles's apartment. We were able to sneak a glance at the interior of the club. As in many other bars, the club was extremely loud with absurd amounts of smoke and lights beaming inside and out. I was able to peek inside briefly at one of the stages. There was a beautiful dancer with the most perfect muscular body dancing in a jockstrap and a matching harness. I couldn't help but think back to the time I danced at Flash, how invigorated I felt dancing all night. But I was on the outside looking in this time. It made me wonder if I ever would be up on that box again. After winding through the streets of Mexico City, I was back at Charles's apartment and in bed within the first half an hour. I was too exhausted to lament negative thoughts about Flash, unemployment, and any other angsty thought that could pop into my head at any moment. I crashed hard and woke up the next day ready to clear my head.

After a brief flight to the East Coast of Mexico, we spent the following few days driving around the Yucatán peninsula in Mexico with our comfortable rental car blasting the air conditioner as high as we could. We zipped around the peninsula chatting in each of our three mutually spoken languages. Charles is another one of those friends with whom I can have endless conversations with and time just flies. We ventured to several beautiful ruins, and I was so lucky to be able to watch Charles show off his indigenous language skills not only to the camera I was holding but also to some locals we encountered along the way.

*Sheesh, he's so smart and so charming. What the hell have you done with your life? Whatever, chill. It's not a contest.*

While the trip was enjoyable, driving in Mexico is now one of my least favorite things to do in the whole world, ranked somewhere up there with root canals and explosive diarrhea. Not only are most of the roads themselves bumpy and unpaved, but there are fun little mechanisms for slowing down speedy drivers. They are called "topes," which translates to speed bumps in English. Unlike most of the speed bumps in the United States, topes are not painted with bright yellow paint. To the dismay of many drivers, these topes frequently pop up suddenly and without any warning whatsoever. You could be having the most pleasant ride of your life in the countryside of Mexico and all of a sudden *bam* now your car is fucked and you have whiplash. I was grumpy to begin with, so sudden bumps in the road popping out of nowhere made me even crankier.

"I swear to god if we hit *one* more of those pinche topes..." I growled bilingually through my teeth.

"Calm yourself, the hotel is just a few blocks away, unless you want me to turn off for another little erotic photoshoot," Charles said.

"I'm going to come back here with a fucking sledgehammer and smash those stupid bumps one by one," I said annoyed.

"Be my guest," he concurred.

"Or couldn't the government at least paint some of these speed bumps? God, is paint really *that* expensive?" I complained.

"I think it's a deterrent for drivers that drive too fast on the highways," he said.

"Well, they should put snipers on the sides of the road and shoot out the tires of bitches that speed," I said.

"Snipers? On the side of the road? Aren't you left-wing?" he asked dryly.

"Of course I am. But I'm also a cranky person that fucking hates these stupid goddamn speed bumps!" I complained with a little more gusto.

It got quiet. We kept driving through the Mexican countryside in silence, not even the radio was playing. I looked outside at the beautiful scenery. There were only a few clouds in the sky, and the sun was shining down brightly on the rugged pavement beneath us. Taking in a few more breaths, I turned over and looked at Charles.

"I'm sorry," I said softly.

"For what?" he asked, confused.

"I'm ruining a nice day by bitching about something I can't—fuck!" I yelled as we hit yet another massive speed bump.

I tried composing myself so as not to contradict my apology.

"I'm sorry for ruining a nice day by bitching about something that I can't even control. You were so sweet to invite me on this trip, and I've been so grumpy," I said.

"Oh, no, you've been fine," he said. "I always enjoy your company, and I find your cantankerous outbursts rather humorous."

I kept forgetting that Charles had been working in government for many years. Working as a bureaucrat, he's probably around depressed, curmudgeonly people every day, so this was probably nothing for him.

*You're still a dick, you're on a free trip to Mexico, ungrateful twat waffle. He's so cute, I don't want him to be mad at me. He's not mad at you, just keep your big, stupid mouth shut, fool.*

The final day of our journey was to the world-famous Chichén Itzá. This was the only site that I knew about when I was invited. We organized a fully packed day to cap off the trip: get up early and head to the site, visit a cenote nearby, and then cap the day off at our hotel for a quiet final evening. It was the perfect balance of adventure and relaxation.

We got to the entrance, and the place was packed with vendors, parking "helpers," and other tourists. When we finally got past the entrance, I was enthralled by the beauty of the ancient site and quite impressed by the preservation of ruins that have been on the planet for over a millennium. We took a lot of photos and did our best to stay out of the sun, which was nearly impossible, but I was thrilled to check off another wonder of the world from my bucket list.

After we made the long journey back to our car in the dusty old parking lot, we headed off to the final cenote of our journey. It wasn't too far away from Chichén Itzá, and there was plenty of parking when we arrived. It was a clothed cenote, but I brought one of my sexy swimsuits.

The vertical cave was surrounded by spiraling stairs that led to a body of water below; it was almost like entering a different world. Vines stretched down from the top of the cave to the bottom, almost as if the cenote had been decorated by gods. Above us, we saw some other tourists cliff diving into the water from a ledge. From the angle we were at as we walked down to the water, the height from which the divers were jumping did not look very high. I decided to give it a go. I was feeling adventurous that day, why not?

"So, who's going first, me or you?" I asked.

"Are you mad? I'm not going to jump, it's far too high for me," Charles said.

"This is exactly why we beat your asses in 1776. No guts, no glory," I responded sarcastically.

Charles rolled his eyes but couldn't help but laugh.

Well, angles are everything. As I walked up the stairs leading to the edge of the cliff, fear began to creep in; it was much higher than I had anticipated. There were three people in front of me, so I was able to see how a jump was done properly. When it was finally my turn, I approached the edge and looked down below. I enjoy the thrill of roller coasters, but only because I am physically strapped in with a seatbelt with a group of other people. Diving alone is a different beast: you are not strapped into anything, and you are completely alone.

I breathed in deeply and closed my eyes. All the pain, frustration, and angst I had felt from the previous few months flashed briefly before my eyes. After taking one more deep breath, I jumped.

I submerged into the water and wanted to stay down there as long as I could stand it or as long as my life jacket would physically allow me to. Something about taking an adventurous plunge, only to be met with a rush of cold water, bubbles, and silence, felt euphoric. After I reached the surface again, I buoyed myself in silence with my head facing up toward the hollow opening of the cenote above me. The sun began to beam and shone the most exquisite ray of light into the cave. I placed my head beneath the surface of the water so that my ears were submerged. I could not hear anything but mere mumblings from the surface above. I watched that big, bright golden ray of light hit the long, green vines that descended to the water.

After reemerging onto the surface, I found Charles waiting on the sidelines.

"How was it?" he inquired.

"I'm glad I did it. And I think you should too," I said.

We shared a laugh and then submerged both of ourselves into the water again. Soaking in the refreshing water on our hot skin that had been baked at the Mayan ruins all week was just what we needed. After a few hours, we were exhausted and ready to drive to our final hotel of the trip.

We checked in a couple of hours before sunset. It was a beautiful spring evening, so we decided to explore some more sites. Unfortunately, everything was closed. Trying to make the best of an already busy and fun day, we drove around the city for a little while. This particular city was very laid back, people seemed very relaxed. Children played in the nearby park while parents sat on the benches. The attitude of the people I saw was what I had been aspiring to be for so many months: content, blissful, and serene.

When we returned an hour or so later, the jacuzzi that was centrally located in the hotel was occupied by a very cute local boy in a very skimpy bikini-cut swimsuit, taking photos of himself. Charles and I immediately looked at each other and giggled slightly; no straight man would ever wear that kind of swimwear alone in a jacuzzi, let alone take photos of himself. Deciding to investigate, we went back into our room and returned to the hot tub in our swimwear.

We struck up a conversation with him in Spanish. Delighted and surprised to see two tourists who could speak Spanish, the handsome young man looked at us with a sense of fascination. We kept tiptoeing around trying to get a hint of his sexual orientation, but he responded with very vague answers. When we started to prune, Charles and I returned to our room.

Once the door was closed, we immediately hopped onto a certain hookup app to see if the scantily clad local was online and nearby.

"He's got to be on here. Ugh, so many notifications!" I exclaimed as I flipped through my phone.

"Scroll past them! We have a mystery to solve," Charles said.

"Cool it, Watson," I joked.

There he was. Online, and nearby. Check and check.

"I fucking knew it!" I exclaimed in a loud whisper, shaking my fist in the air victoriously.

"He's so charming! Do you think he would fancy a visit over here?" Charles asked.

"We're going to find out right about now," I laughed as I sent our new amigo a message inviting him to join us in the hotel room.

It didn't take long for him to respond. The handsome guest, Juan, happened to be visiting this little town on vacation. He indicated to us that he was on a "don't ask, don't tell" basis with his travel companions but was eager to join Charles and me in the bedroom. He only had fifteen minutes, so we were ready to get started as soon as he arrived in our room. It seemed like a crazy idea to all three of us, and yet we proceeded.

After sneaking into our room, Charles and I slowly stripped our guest down to his very skimpy underwear. I was in front of Juan, kissing him, and Charles was behind him, grabbing his crotch with one hand and his rear end with the other. I began to kiss Juan passionately on the neck as he slowly turned around and began to make out with Charles. I slid Juan's tight briefs down and began to squeeze his buttocks, which were so tight and smooth. I began to get hard. Pulling Juan by the waist closer to me, I picked him up and threw his slender body onto his back on the bed. Sliding my hard-on into his mouth and running my fingers through his soft hair, Charles came up behind me and started servicing Juan.

I rubbed Juan's hard nipples with the tips of my thumbs, which made him moan quietly.

"Buen chico," I whispered as I kissed his neck passionately. "Asi es, chico."

After pulling out of his mouth, I flipped Juan over on his back and forced him onto all fours. I started to rub his butt check and let in some nice firm spanks to show I meant business. Charles went around and put his bulging erection into Juan's mouth. Charles and I started making out as I rubbed my erection between the cheeks of a beautiful smooth ass that now had my red handprints all over it.

We proceeded to roll around in various positions, touching and making out, before I climaxed in Juan's mouth.

"Buen hecho, chico," I whispered as I stroked his soft, wavy black hair and gave his face a few light taps.

Charles came all over himself from behind us, watching Juan finish me off. We were all panting as Juan climaxed into a towel while on his stomach. After quietly slipping his clothes back on, he left our room as quickly as a mouse.

Finally recovering our breaths, Charles and I looked at each other and immediately burst into laughter.

"Um, what just happened?" I asked rhetorically.

"I don't know! What a pleasant surprise that was!" Charles said as we both continued to laugh.

"That was so hot. Damn, I should have brought my inhaler," I said, panting.

"Don't have a heart attack! We're quite far from the nearest hospital!" he joked.

"You know what? Fuck it. Let's go get a pizza!" I suggested enthusiastically as I finished cleaning myself up.

"Ok!" Charles said, laughing emphatically.

We walked out of that hotel like we had just won the lottery with locked arms and all smiles from ear to ear. I suggested that we take a selfie while the dreamy looks on our faces were still fresh. Whipping my phone out, I scrolled past the notifications on my phone so that I could take a selfie with Charles. Our faces still looked so dreamy.

Despite all the notifications on my phone from all my postings, I wanted to remain present in the moment, so I put my phone in Airplane Mode.

We walked down the streets so carefree, not even talking. It was the kind of happy where you don't want to be anywhere else. Unlike previous months, getting out felt like a liberating adventure and not a burdensome chore.

*Am I getting better? Could this trip be a turning point?*

When we got to the pizza place, we were informed that it would be a nearly 45-minute wait for our pizza. Desperate for this savory meal to cap off an already awesome day, we decided to endure the wait. Fortunately for us, there was a zócalo just outside the pizza place. That night, there happened to be some kind of festival, so there was a giant stage supporting a very talented live band and accentuated by colorful lights beaming in all directions. We walked out and saw a crowd of happy people dancing to the beat of the music. We meandered through the park to people-watch. There were tons of happy families, children, and young couples all dancing together and enjoying the night out.

As we got closer to the stage at the front of the park, we saw a group of Mexican women wearing bike helmets. Approaching even closer, we saw that they were dancing together in front of a row of bikes. Upon asking in Spanish why they had bikes, the ladies immediately widened their eyes with surprise that we could speak Spanish. The group huddled around us, grabbed both our hands, pulled us to the dance floor, and started dancing with us.

*Guess we're not going to get the answer to our questions. Whatever, let's dance.*

They were not trying to impress anyone, nor was I. Charles, however, was able to show off some of the skills that he had learned in a salsa class earlier that year, and I was able to gyrate and dance like I had back in Fresno. Both of our moves were met with whistling and hollering from the other women. They began high-fiving us every time we performed a move.

We were so sweaty from dancing, but that didn't stop us from hugging every single one of the women and squishing in for a group photo. We would later learn that these women had biked from Cancún and that the city we were in was one of their last stops. After taking one final photo and a few more selfies with individual cyclists, we went to the pizza shop to retrieve our warm, cheesy prize for the day and headed back to the hotel.

Eating that first slice of pizza was a fantastic cherry on top of a terrific day. I was elated and in awe that over a period of 12 hours, I was able to see one of the seven wonders of the world, face my fears by jumping from a cliff at a stunning cenote, have an incredibly hot serendipitous encounter with my friend and a hot local, and now I was about to cap off the day with a delicious slice of pizza. All things considered, it was all I wanted at that moment. I didn't want anything extravagant or extra; I just wanted some carbs and cheesy Italian goodness.

Feeling slightly verklempt, I looked Charles right in the eye.

"Thank you so much," I said earnestly.

"For what?" Charles said, with a mouth full of pizza.

"For being such an attractive dinner companion, you weirdo," I laughed back, gesturing for him to wipe the tomato sauce from his chin. "I'm sorry for being kind of cranky earlier this week. It's just been ten months of seemingly non-stop bullshit."

"Are you referring to your job situation?" he asked.

"Job situation. Self-esteem. Lack of direction. Drinking myself to sleep. And, of course, the depressive spiral," I said.

"Well, at least the videos you send me at midnight are entertaining," he said.

"I appreciate that. Honestly, I think when I get back home, I'm going to start cutting down on the drinking, so try to get your fill of goofy drunk videos from somebody else," I joked.

"That's good!" he said proudly.

"Not quitting cold turkey, I still need a little buzz once in a while. But now that my libido is creeping back, I think I can go back to just being a social drinker," I said.

"Smashing," he said, making me giggle.

*I freaking love British accents.*

"Thank you very much, poppet," I said, holding up an imaginary teacup with my pinky raised.

"You're incorrigible," he said, laughing.

"Oh, am I? Oh, bloody hell!" I said with an obnoxious cockney accent.

We started howling with laughter. Charles and I had very different senses of humor, but he found it funny that I found his accent and colloquialisms so funny.

"Ok, picture time. I need to remind myself of this moment the next time I feel shitty," I said.

"Your phone or mine?" Charles asked.

"We can do mine," I said as I opened the camera app.

After ensuring that my hair was orderly and the pizza was all out on display, I snapped a photo of the two of us together. For months, I had been smiling for the camera with a fake smile, but not this time.

"Oh, I like this one! Let me just get out of Airplane Mode real quick. I'm going to post this one, is that alright with you?" I asked, showing Charles the pictures.

"Sure!" he said.

I proceeded to open my phone to post the photo. After my phone reconnected to the internet, I went to my social media feed. Instantly, it became clear why I had so many notifications.

Damien was dead.

I froze.

"What is it?" Charles asked.

Unable to react to the shock, I stayed frozen. The only thing I could feel was my heartbeat rising faster and faster. It started in my chest and then led to my face. I could actually feel my neck and face pulsating. I began to huff very brief, sharp breaths.

"DJ? DJ? For heaven's sake, DJ?" Charles asked, snapping his finger in front of me.

My eyes moved up and met his.

"What on earth is the matter?" he asked.

Staring blankly ahead at Charles, nostrils flaring, I finally strung a sentence together.

"Damien. It's Damien. He's dead. He's...he's gone," I muttered, unable to believe the words coming out of my mouth.

"Oh, oh no," Charles responded, not knowing what to say.

I paused again, completely frozen and in complete shock. We sat that way for a few more seconds.

"What happened?" Charles asked.

Upon skimming through the announcement on Gavin's profile, I was able to learn what had happened.

"Heart attack," I said.

"That's so dreadful," Charles said, unsure how to comport himself.

I knew Damien had struggled with anxiety and had been trying to quit smoking for years. He had a stressful job and didn't exercise often. But this was so sudden, I couldn't believe it. I refused to believe it.

"Ok, Charles, I need to tell you this right now because I know I have a very short window of time to be able to say this: I am going to be behaving like this for about 10 minutes. Then I am going to start crying uncontrollably. Please don't say anything, just hold me whenever I start crying. That's how I process grief, got it? Shock first, then tears, and a lot of different feelings after. I just need you to know that," I said.

"Ok," Charles said with a nod.

We just sat there for several minutes. I stared into space.

Instantly, my brain went into a reel of all the moments Damien and I had shared over the past two years. Meeting him at a party, having a drink with him and Gavin every time I came home to visit, dancing around Gavin's living room to old records, and especially, the first time I ever go-go danced. I thought long and deeply about that moment when everyone else was dancing and in their own little world, I looked over at Damien, and he gave me the look. That look. That motherfucking look. All I could think about was that exact moment at Flash. It was like I had paused a movie, and that was all I could look at. His face. My beautiful Damien's face. I was never going to see that face again.

With that already emotionally tender thought in my head, I stared directly into Charles's eyes. My nostrils flared more heavily as my heart began to beat faster and faster. Staring back at me without blinking, Charles reached his hand out and touched mine. That's when I broke down. I began to sob uncontrollably. The shock was over, and the grief began to set in. I had not seen Damien in several weeks. I never said goodbye.

After ten minutes of non-stop sobbing, I was able to catch my breath and compose myself. I wiped away the flood of tears that had stained my face and looked at Charles.

"Where's the nearest fucking liquor store?" I mumbled firmly through my gritted teeth.

*Here you go again. Always drowning out your pain in alcohol. Shut the fuck up, my best friend just died, I will drink whatever I goddamn well, please. Ok, suit yourself, fucker.*

"Let's go. I'll search for one on my phone," Charles said, reaching out his hand for mine again. Still in a state of grief, Charles had to put in extra effort to pull me out of my chair. My chest began to tighten, and I had to consciously pace my breathing. He held me up with one arm and searched where to find the nearest liquor store with the other.

After walking several paces outside of the hotel entrance, I suddenly dropped to my knees like a sack of flour and started dry heaving on the sidewalk. No vomit was coming out, but with every heave, I felt the muscles in my abdomen, oblique muscles, and back stretch to their limits. I was beginning to feel severe pain in my ribcage. All I felt was uncontrollable pain coursing its way through my body.

I was too hysterical to go inside, so Charles helped me sit down on a bench outside the store where I could let all my feelings out. He walked in to buy us some vodka, and I just sat there on the bench alone.

*Did this all happen in one day? The same day, I went to one of the seven wonders of the world? The same day I jumped off a cliff inside a gorgeous cenote? The same day that one of my closest friends of mine and I had a hot threesome with a cute local? The same day we danced the night away with a group of fabulously fun ladies who were cheering us on and loving every minute? The same day when all I had to do was go home and cap it off with a nice, delicious pizza? This could not have happened on the same day. Son of a bitch. Fuck. This. Shit.*

The emotions swirled in a messy, sporadic vortex that began to feel very disorienting. As much as I tried not to think about Damien, he was all I could think about. The tears gushed out like a geyser, and I was not able to hold myself upright. Right at the exact moment when I was starting to feel better, right as I was ready to *document* myself feeling better, life had delivered me the biggest possible bitch slap. I was gutted.

Charles returned with a bottle of vodka and used his other arm to pick me up and help me back to the hotel. It took all the effort I could possibly muster to avoid collapsing and dry heaving again. We finally got back to the hotel, and I drank the vodka straight from the bottle.

"Are you sure you don't want a chaser?" he asked, gesturing towards the half-empty bottle of sodas in our backpacks. I couldn't respond verbally, so I just wagged my finger. After consuming about 3 to 4 gulps of vodka, I stripped naked and jumped into bed. Charles did the same and joined me.

I stared up at the ceiling, allowing the alcohol to enter my system and numb my shattered heart.

"What can I do to help now?" Charles inquired sheepishly.

"You're here. That's all the help I need right now," I said.

"Ok. Do you want to talk at all?" Charles asked.

"I guess," I said.

We talked for a while about Damien. All the memories. All the crazy antics we got into with Gavin. Bizarrely enough, I was able to muster up a few genuine laughs as I reflected on certain memories. Whether or not that was because of the humor in the anecdotes or the vodka is anybody's guess.

One particular story involved me, Gavin, and Damien being very silly late at night when I was visiting from graduate school. Gavin had a record player in his home with hundreds of vinyl records, which included recordings of several Broadway musicals. He and I started tickling each other and reenacted the "Lonely Goatherd" scene from *The Sound of Music*. I grabbed Gavin's wrists from behind and lifted them up and down like a puppet while Damien recorded us. We all laughed so hard at that story when it happened, and would laugh at it anytime it was brought up again. As I started laughing, my tears of laughter began to blend in with my tears of sorrow. After laughing for a good several minutes, the tears went back to those of sadness. All those happy memories were just memories now. I would never have a night like that with Damien and Gavin ever again.

When I felt my blood pressure and feelings boiling up again, I took another swig of vodka. Charles rubbed my back as I turned sideways on the bed. After a few minutes, I could hear his phone notifications buzzing; the pinging from one particular hookup app kept coming up. With his other hand that wasn't rubbing my back, he picked up the phone.

"Hey, Juan wants to come back again for round two, but I'm going to tell him no," Charles said.

Damien had responded to a few of my vacation photos from this trip just a few days earlier. I knew as soon as I came back home, he would have wanted to hear about all of my sexy, fun adventures. He would have loved to hear about the rest of my trip, but he definitely would have wanted to hear about the spontaneous threesome first. I know without a shadow of a doubt that he would have wanted me to go round two, but given the state I was in, Charles made the right decision.

"Why did I think I was going to get better?" I said aloud as Charles turned off his phone.

"What do you mean?" he asked.

"I mean that for the first time in a very long time, I was starting to feel good again. Good about myself, and hopeful for the future. It felt good to be out, good to be around people. And then I got hit by a freaking bus. Is this going to keep happening? I don't know how much more of this I can take," I slurred.

"I know. This hasn't been a great few months for you," Charles said as he continued to rub my back.

"I should just stop trying to be happy. From now on, I'm going to cap my happiness level at 30%," I declared.

"What do you mean?"

"I mean that on a scale of 1 to 100, 1 being the least happy and 100 being happy as a clam, I am going to not allow myself to go beyond a 30. It's dangerous," I said.

"Oh, I see what you mean," Charles responded in a manner that conveyed that he knew what I meant and disagreed, but did not want to push back at all against what I was saying. I told you Charles was a smart man.

After drinking a little more of my massive nightcap, I fell asleep. I do not remember falling asleep, but I do remember waking up. I don't get hangovers really, but this was a worse wake-up call. My chest woke me up. It was so unbearably tight. I began to sob uncontrollably, again, upon realizing that the news of Damien's passing had not been a dream.

As much as I tried to keep quiet, I had woken Charles up. He immediately began rubbing my back.

"I'm so sorry," I said through tears as he tried his best to calm me down.

"You did nothing wrong," Charles assured.

*This has to be rock bottom, right? There's no way I can keep getting bad news after bad news after bad news. I've never had alcohol this early in the morning, but I guess there's a first time for everything.*

I cried for about a full hour early that morning before falling in and out of sleep. Lying there in the darkness underneath the covers, I did not want to move from the little cocoon I had made with the sheets. Then, I felt a tap on my head.

"Hey there, good morning, again," Charles said in a soft tone. "Sorry to wake you, but it is check-out time and they're going to charge us extra if we don't leave."

I scowled but managed to uncover myself. The harsh, blinding light that awaited me stung for a good thirty seconds. I'm not a morning person at all, but it was time to go. I took another few swigs of the vodka before I started packing up my stuff.

We made our way to the airport, but since we arrived much earlier than I had anticipated, we had a lot of time to kill before both of our flights back home. We found a restaurant that was within walking distance of the airport that had some cute little benches outside. We sat on the benches and I continued feeling the worst feelings in the world. Still not believing that Damien was gone, I was once again filled with a deep sense of hopelessness.

*What am I going back home to? What's even the point of going back home? When will this fucking nightmare end? Hell, I'd rather go back to the toucan nightmare at this point. Was that pizza selfie the last time I will ever feel that happy again?*

"Are you going to be ok?" Charles asked.

*How am I supposed to answer that question? Just answer honestly. No, don't do that. He's going to call the cops on your drunk ass if you tell him the truth.*

"Maybe someday," I said back.

I hugged Charles much longer than I would have when we exchanged goodbyes, then I began to tear up. I didn't want to let him go; it felt like I was giving Charles the goodbye hug that I was never able to give Damien. But it was time to go, so I got on the plane and flew back north.


Driving home from the San Diego side of the Tijuana airport was surreal. As I made my way through classic Southern California traffic, I slapped myself in the face multiple times, hoping to wake up from this nightmare I was living. The more I tried that, the more I failed.

Wanting to drown out the sorrow with music, Lady Gaga's song "Hold My Hand" coincidentally began to play on the radio. The chorus is powerful and struck a very firm chord with me. I ended up having to pull over on the side of the road because I was not able to see through the tears. I struggled, but I managed to sing along to the final chorus as loudly as I possibly could. By singing, mind you, I mean halfway between singing and screaming; I felt like I was screaming into an endless void.

When I arrived back at my parents' house in Visalia late that afternoon, I sat in the car for a good ten minutes. I didn't want to get out, I was still in denial. When I left this spot, Damien was still alive. Now, he was gone.

*Don't get out of the car, it's an admission that he's dead. He's already dead. He's not coming back; getting out of the car isn't going to change that. Deal with it.*

Taking a few more deep breaths, I got out of the car and walked into the house. My parents were already in the kitchen awaiting my arrival. They both greeted me by sandwiching me into a hug. This, of course, made me cry even more. I collapsed to the floor, again, and they followed me down. I sobbed uncontrollably into my mom's shoulder. My dad massaged my back while my mom began to weep with me.

*Here we are again, another meltdown on the kitchen floor.*

I finally pulled myself together and looked up at my parents.

"What do you need from us?" my mom asked.

"I don't know. I really don't know," I said, wiping away the tears. "I just would like for all of this to stop."

We just sat there together in silence for a few minutes. I managed not to cry again by taking a series of very deep breaths. Breathe in, breathe out.

"What do you want to do now?" my dad asked me.

Both my parents stared at me intently as I contemplated the path before me. On the one hand, I was still unemployed, jaded as all hell, pissed off, and now the depression I had already been struggling with was mutating into absolute despair by the unexpected death of a dear friend. On the other hand, that same dear friend who always listened to my rants, always held me when he knew I was feeling bad, was now forever etched into my psyche. As he lingered in my heart and soul, I asked myself a simple question.

*What would Damien want me to do right now?*

As I stared blankly ahead, contemplating my parents' existential question, I could see Damien's face again; his beautiful, handsome face beaming back at me just as he did at Flash that night. I knew in that moment that I only had two options: I could either keep drinking heavily and possibly develop my own health problems in addition to spiraling even more out of control, or I could take my grief out at the gym and work even harder than I had before. As I contemplated this question, it was clear to me what Damien would have wanted: he would have wanted me to be happy, healthy, and get really sexy in the process. Damien loved life, joy, and beauty. That's what he would have wanted, so I knew what I had to do.

"I'm going to the gym," I said to my parents. And with that, we shared one final long group hug in the kitchen. I went to my room to get changed, and immediately drove to the gym and stayed there for two long hours.

I would later learn that Damien had actually died earlier that day, before Charles and I had arrived at Chichén Itzá. I'm not a big believer in destiny or fate, but something about this did give me pause. He died right before my near-perfect day in Mexico. What if I had found out about his death that morning? The whole day, all the amazing things I was able to do probably wouldn't have happened. There is no way in hell I would have even been able to go to Chichén Itzá, the cenote, the hotel sexy time, or the fabulous park afterward with that kind of burden on my heart and soul. Perhaps that was Damien's parting gift to me: letting me enjoy one final fabulous day in the sun before the unbearable weight of grief of his passing hit me out of fucking nowhere, just like a "tope" on the highways of Mexico.

# CHAPTER 7

## WHAT WAS I MADE FOR?

By the summer of 2023, I wondered if the string of bad luck was just an infinite loop. I continued to apply online to any random job I could find. I returned to the same old routine: wake up around noon, go to the gym, apply for jobs, drink, go to sleep. I successfully faked my way through Mother's Day and my birthday, but that happy mask kept getting heavier and heavier.

As distraught as I was, I stumbled upon two small glimmers of hope as spring turned into summer. The first was an offer from my theater friends to write an original murder mystery play for the theater company. Since there are now a million forms of cheap entertainment, streaming services, and mind-numbing apps, small-town theater companies are struggling to get regular audiences in seats. Virtual entertainment is accessible, popular, and cheap, but as a result, traditional forms of entertainment like live theater have been left behind. These are the types of activities that hold communities together, so I was happy to rise to the occasion.

All I was given was a title, a genre, and a few months to finish the play before auditions were held. Having a project to work on did not stop the spiraling, but it did give me a creative, constructive outlet to occupy my time. The amount of time I spent languishing all day was reduced by an hour or two, where I could create, write, and focus my attention on something fulfilling.

The second glimmer of hope emerged when I received an email with a job offer to work on a campaign in Jackson, Mississippi. The job was essentially the lowest-ranking official on the campaign staff, the base of the shaft, if you will. But I knew this was not the time to complain; at least I could add *something* to my stupid resume.

My parents were overjoyed when I told them the news, but their enthusiasm eclipsed mine by a mile. Breaking out of the negative mindset felt impossible; the cycle of despair, especially on the employment front, meant that my default was to hope for the mediocre and expect the worst.

The first thing I did after accepting the offer was to look at the accommodation. The second thing I did was to look at the nightlife situation. The Deep South is obviously very conservative, but the big cities within it, in my experience, usually have a surprisingly vibrant nightlife. Hoping to make some side money to compensate for the low pay rate at the campaign, I reached out to the main gay bar in Jackson to ask if they had any opportunities for part-time work on the side, including dancing. I didn't receive a response, which I was more than used to by then.

My very helpful father, always down for a road trip, helped me pack up my bags and drove with me all the way from California to Mississippi. We spent most of the road trip listening to music, discussing current events, and making silly jokes. My dad and I are extremely similar in personality, and both have a very bizarre sense of humor that very few people can understand. This helped make the unbearably long journey across the states even more bearable.

Unable to find temporary accommodation, I managed to find a long-term stay hotel relatively close to the campaign headquarters. It was located just off the highway and reeked of weed and urine. I got out of the car, reluctantly checked in, and was shown to my room, a very small studio on the first floor with a modest-sized kitchenette.

The cicadas in the Deep South are deafening and omnipresent. The humidity is as bad as people say it is, and the poverty of the entire region is felt in nearly every corner of the city. This is not the place I ever imagined myself living, but at least it was a job, a paycheck, and a path forward to a career in public policy.

My dad took me on a grocery store run and filled my fridge with food before I had to take him to the airport. Driving down the highway back to my very dilapidated hotel, reality began to set in again: this was where I would be living for the next five months. The night before my first day of orientation, I wanted to scope out the local singles, so I hopped onto one of the apps and began browsing.

I ended up finding a very handsome local cutie named Darnell. He was a couple of years younger than me, but had the most attractive smile and an even more attractive rear end. I invited him over to hang out; if I was going to stay here through November, I was at least going to meet *one* person I could spend time with after I clocked out.

He approached the door, and I invited him in. Since I was new to Jackson and the whole Deep South in general, he gave me the lay of the land. What he described absolutely horrified me. Granted, Darnell was African-American, so much of what he said was coming from his experience and would not necessarily apply to me as well.

"Here, you're going to need this," he said.

"Uh, is that a switchblade?" I asked.

"Yeah," he said, placing it in my right hand.

"And why would I need this?" I asked with an awkward laugh.

"You need to protect yourself out here; you can never be too safe," he said without laughing.

*Yeah, that's comforting coming from a stranger I invited over to my hotel room.*

"Um, Darnell, is that...is that a confederate flag on the side of the knife?" I said, pointing to the side of the knife, which displayed a very faded stars and bars.

"Oh, huh, I never noticed that. Yeah, probably, I don't know. I got it at a yard sale," he said indifferently.

"Uh-huh, I see. And was this yard sale at a rally with a burning cross? Get that thing away from me. What will the hotel employees think if they see me with this?" I asked, alarmed.

"Out here, we're just surviving," he said.

His blunt manner of speaking and indifference towards the symbol etched on the side of the knife threw me completely off balance. That last part, though, about surviving, sounded particularly ominous; I felt like I was entering the Twilight Zone.

*Am I really in that much danger?*

"Ok, well, could you survive out here with a knife that doesn't carry the flag of sore losers?" I said, laughing very uncomfortably.

*What. The. Actual. Fuck.*

He chuckled a bit as he tried to calm me down. We began talking about his childhood, which was not positive. I learned about the areas of town to stay away from, what to do if people made me uncomfortable, and where to avoid, especially after sundown. Grateful though I was that he was disclosing all of this useful information, I became more depressed as the night went on. This was going to be my new reality for about half a year. Trying to change the subject, I asked him about gay nightlife. That answer was depressing, too.

Darnell happened to moonlight as a drag queen at the only gay bar in town. He told me that they did not hire go-go dancers, and they barely paid the drag queens they *did* have. This realization did not help with the subject and mood change I had anticipated, so I just started making out with Darnell. The best way to help myself forget the gloomy reality he had laid out for me was to squeeze his firm, juicy glutes. It did not change the reality of the game, but it helped me tap out of reality for a few moments.

We cuddled for a bit longer before Darnell had to go home. I fell into bed staring at the ceiling, all the positive feelings I felt making out with Darnell and grabbing his ass began to recede as I processed the wave of warnings he had given me. I was instructed by a local to carry a switchblade with me, not talk to strangers, stay inside after the sun goes down, and not have a fun gay bar to blow off steam after work. Also, I formulated a plan to get rid of *this* particular knife first thing the next morning and get one without *that* flag on it.

*Having fun yet? Is this what you worked so hard to achieve? You wanted a job, didn't you? Yes, but this is way too much to handle, and on the first night?*

*There's always alcohol, and you know that makes you feel better. Yes, but it also is not healthy and makes me feel like crap the next morning. Well, speaking of morning, you should probably pop a melatonin and go to sleep. You get to start your super awesome job tomorrow. Night night, fuck face.*

Orientation was incredibly boring and very uncomfortable. For one, the positive, upbeat attitude of the staff on our Zoom meeting belied the dire warnings I had been given by Darnell the night before; I have still to this day never been more uncomfortable starting a new job than that first day in Jackson.

Making matters more uncomfortable, my new boss, who was around my age, took an interest in me early on. At first, I just thought he was being polite, but after a while, I had the same uncomfortable feeling in the pit of my stomach that I had in Palm Springs; I could feel him looking at me in inappropriate ways when he thought I wasn't looking. Due to my lack of self-esteem at that point, I felt flattered and didn't know how to establish healthy workplace boundaries. I felt stuck in an awkward position between appreciating the confidence boosting compliments and wanting to be seen as a team member with skills to contribute. The unprofessional compliments kept coming but I didn't know how to stop them; after all, he did promise to employ his political connections to help me find a job eventually.

A few days later, a massive thunderstorm hit the state; lightning flashed brightly and thunder boomed throughout the Deep South. Still not feeling great in the self-esteem department, I tried to get my mind off things by taking some naked photos in the mirror and sending them to friends; that's when the power went off.

*Goddammit. Not again.*

I turned on my flashlight on my phone to try to figure out what the hell was going on. As it turned out, over half the city had lost power. Darnell texted me when he got home to tell me that the power went out at his place, too. The battery on my phone only had 30% or so remaining, so I called my parents.

"Hey there, working boy! How was your first day at your new job?" my mom asked, pleasantly.

*So fucking peachy, mommy dearest. Let's see: my boss is a fucking creep, the place I live now is so dangerous that a local boy thinks I should carry around a switchblade with me, and I lost power after less than a week. But other than that, Mrs. Lincoln, how was the play?*

"Everything is…going to shit," I said, bluntly.

"What's wrong? And what's that noise? It's kind of hard to hear you," she responded, concerned.

Trying my utmost to not blow a gasket, I told her that I had lost power, that the hundreds of dollars' worth of groceries I had in the fridge were going to be ruined, and tried to calmly tell her I did not feel the safest in the area I was in; I didn't have the heart to tell her about the switchblade.

After a few minutes, I could hear my dad in the background calling up every hotel in Jackson to see if they had power so I could have a place to rest with functioning A/C and charge my phone for work the next day.

"Hold up, my boss just texted me. He said most of the city has lost power, but he hasn't yet, and now he's offering me to crash on his couch," I said.

"We will keep calling hotels and let you know, I'm so sorry, sweetheart. This doesn't seem like a great way to start your new job," she said.

After several hours on the phone with multiple hotels, it was clear that every single one of them was booked. I walked over to my kitchenette, took a few more shots of vodka, and got down on my back; lying flat on the floor in a powerless room felt like the perfect metaphor. The temperature in the room began to rise as it was a hot summer in the Deep South with no A/C. The battery in my phone was beginning to approach the single digits. At that point, I had a choice to make: I could either sleep in my 89-degree hotel room with a switchblade under my pillow or take my boss up on his offer to sleep on his couch for the night until the power came back on.

I chose the latter. Later that night, while I was drunk, my boss took advantage of me. That's all I will say about that.

So I left Jackson.

.   .   .

*Good mother fucking riddance to this whole shit experience.*

Driving north on the highway felt riveting at first. Apart from meeting Darnell, a complete gem of a human being, every single thing about my experience in Jackson was horrible. I felt huge relief for leaving that miserable job, and was proud of getting myself into a negative situation, but then pulling myself out of it. I lowered the windows and blasted out Pink's "So What" on repeat. I may or may not have screamed some expletives out the window.

After a few minutes of riding the contradictory wave of pure angst and utter jubilation, I rolled the windows back up and reality reared its ugly head.

*You're going to be so fucking broke dude. You should have just sucked it up and kept working there, dumbass. You can barely hold employment for a couple of weeks, you're destined to be out of work and unemployed forever. Just go do a PhD. Lots of miserable people do that! No, fat chance. I'm still exhausted from the degree I finished last year. Move back to Asia, that's where the hot boys are. No, go back to Palm Springs. Sell your kidney. Rob a bank.*

To drown out my inner thoughts, I picked some podcasts to listen to. I had no idea where exactly I was driving, but I had already planned to attend Kiana's wedding in Colorado Springs later that week. Since I had friends and family in Denver, that seemed like the best possible refuge I could make out of a crappy situation.

Enrique, who had been living in Denver for the past few months, offered to host me at his apartment. In addition, he invited me to be his plus one to a series of events he was attending with politicians, donors, and well-connected people. Enrique was a safe person I could trust to make me feel supported and secure. I arrived in Denver after a few days crossing through the middle of the country.

The first few nights after I arrived, we attended a lot of events together. Some casual, others black tie only. After a crazy few days of attempted networking, the cynicism I had been feeling reached new heights. I ended up spending a lot of time alone in Enrique's apartment with all the lights turned off. I didn't want to be anywhere else but the lowest possible place in the room, so I would often find myself lying on the floor wishing that there was a lower level where I could sink.

Putting the happy mask back on, I attended Kiana's wedding in Colorado Springs a few days later. My entire family seemed to be walking on eggshells around me. This was a happy occasion that I didn't want to ruin by unloading everything that had happened the previous couple of weeks. In my family, I have a reputation as the funny cousin, but everyone had at least some knowledge that I was going through something and was not being myself. Trying to fake a smile for joyous occasions was getting more and more difficult. Even on the dance floor of the wedding, all I could think about was going back to Enrique's apartment and lying flat on the ground.

I returned to Denver the day after the wedding. Enrique told me to meet him in the jacuzzi when I returned.

"Hey! Look who's bringing sexy back! How was the wedding? Did you have a fabulous time?" he asked as I entered the hot tub.

"I faked my way through most of it. So, I guess that means it was a successful weekend," I said.

"Did you pick up any cute bartenders?" he joked.

"No, but I sure enjoyed their drinks," I said.

"Well, in other news, what did you think of last week?" Enrique asked.

"I think Denver is a lucky city to have you in it," I said.

"Aww, that's not what I meant, but thank you! I meant, what did you think of the parties? Did you get any leads on jobs?" he inquired, sensing that I was holding something back.

"I don't think I want to work in politics anymore," I said bluntly.

"Wait, what?! Why? Because of what happened in Jackson?" he asked, shocked.

"It's not just that. I loved volunteering with you last fall. I had a lot of fun and felt like I was a part of something. But actually working in politics, I don't know, I felt shitty about myself, the country, and frankly the whole human race. Seeing things up close behind the scenes, seeing how the sausage gets made, just makes me not want to work in this business," I said.

"Well, what about working in politics makes you feel shitty about the human race?" he asked with a little chuckle.

"Well, like that black-tie party we went to the other night. I had a great time when we were just hanging around your coworkers, almost all of them were perfectly lovely. People at that after-party were perfectly polite and friendly too, but as soon as they asked who invited me, they immediately started throwing their business cards in my face and asking me for your phone number. Not my phone number, your phone number," I said. "I don't think access to these kinds of people is going to help me at all, and I'm done trying."

"Wow, they wanted *my* phone number? If only I had that kind of luck on the dating apps," Enrique joked.

"Anyways. I knew this business wasn't pleasant, but seeing how unpleasant it is up close, I just don't think it's for me. My idealism is all but gone, and I don't like feeling how I felt working on the campaign," I said.

"Well, you've got to have fun with that sexy local boy at least. Did you keep his yard sale knife?" Enrique asked, jokingly.

"Yeah, it's in my gym bag right now," I said sarcastically.

"Really?" he said, feigning credulity.

"No, dumbass, I did not keep that fucking knife, are you insane?" I clapped back.

"Damn. I guess I'll have to find another knife to chase your former boss around with," Enrique said with a little giggle.

*I love him so much, even when he's being a twat.*

"Ok, I'm starting to prune, I'm going to need to get out and bring the rest of my stuff in," I said.

I got out of the jacuzzi, averting my butt cheeks away from Enrique so that he couldn't slap them, and put a towel on. After drying off and putting on some shorts and a tank top, I went outside to return the rest of my wedding attire from my car.

The second I hit the unlock button, a man in a black hoodie and ski mask leaped from the driver's seat inside my car and began running for his life up the street. Just as I had in New York with the intern or in Mississippi with my boss, I just froze and didn't say anything. I felt anger and rage coursing throughout my body, and yet I felt completely immobile.

*Ok, so maybe rock bottom isn't a single destination but rather a massive hell-like basement with plenty of rooms in it to explore.*

Enrique and I filed a police report, but there wasn't much they could do. Fortunately, the bastard didn't steal anything, and as far as I could tell, I don't think he could have gotten away with much. Yes. Sorry not sorry, but Fatass McBurglar deserved that insult.

To blow off some steam from the previous few weeks, I needed to get to a club with my clothes mostly off and let loose. Every Monday night, to encourage more patronage, one of the most popular gay bars in Denver, Chuckie's, offered free drinks to customers who arrived in just their underwear. The weather was still warm, so meandering around in my skivvies was fine by me.

Enrique and I got to the bar just before ten, when the underwear portion of the night started. Wanting to remain discreet, Enrique kept his clothes on while I stripped down to my underwear. I ordered a Dirty Shirley, and Enrique ordered a Diet Ginger Ale. We began making our rounds in the club.

"Can you get me some of *their* business cards, pretty please?" Enrique joked, referring to a sexy gaggle of gays. "Why don't you wear those sexy white Andrew Christian undies? You look so sexy in those!"

"They don't show enough skin," I joked back.

We ended up outside, where it was still relatively warm. I tried as best I could to relax and try to forget about the previous week as much as I could, but it was hard to get out of my negative thoughts. After chatting about the debt ceiling for a few minutes, we were both approached by a handsome blonde twink wearing a colorful neon jock strap. He introduced himself to us as Sean, and he was, as I would soon find out, an employee at Chuckie's who was there on his night off.

The three of us began chatting about life in Denver, local and national politics, and the heat. After a while, Sean began to ask me slightly more pointed personal questions about my current living situation. I replied that my life was essentially in limbo and that I had no official plans, no set goals, and nothing to lose, essentially.

After chatting with Enrique and I for a while, Sean excused himself to make a phone call. Standing just behind Enrique, I could pick out some of the words, and it sounded like he was talking to this guy about me and how I looked. My suspicions were elevated when Sean made eye contact with me.

"Hey, sorry, you live in Denver, right?" Sean asked.

"I'm crashing here currently, yes," I replied.

After a brief squint conveying mild skepticism, Sean replied to the mysterious caller.

"He said he's going to," he said.

*What is even going on here? Am I being followed? Is this a hit man? Is there a connection between this guy and the asshole that broke into my car last week? Ok, stop being paranoid.*

Sean hung up the phone and presented me with a blunt proposal.

"So, just curious, do you have any interest in auditioning to go-go dance here?" he asked.

In the few microseconds after Sean had offered me the opportunity to audition at Chuckie's, I immediately had a flashback to my horrible moment in New York and how disappointed I felt. After ten years of working hard on my brain, I'd had to spend well over a year *begging* for a good-paying job where I could use my academic skills. And now, here I was showing up in my underwear at a bar, and after not even 15 minutes standing here, I was being asked to try out to be a go-go dancer. At long last, I could use my economics training: the invisible hand of the free market was guiding me somewhere else.

*Follow the money, queen. This might be your career. Public policy, academia, and campaigns might not be for you. Maybe it's time to rethink. Don't give up on your other skills, but maybe certain qualities of yours are more sought out now than others.*

"Hello?" Sean said, waving his hand in front of my face to break my daydream.

"Sorry, my bad, low blood sugar," I lied. "I mean, yeah, what does the process look like?"

"Well, we had a dancer call in sick tonight. That was my boss on the phone just now. He said if you're interested in dancing tonight, it'd be like a little audition. We can't pay you anything, but you could keep all of your tips and, if you do well, we might be able to book you," Sean said. "What do you think?"

Enrique was giving me the biggest shit-eating grin in my peripheral vision, trying to nonverbally communicate as emphatically as he could that I should take Sean up on his offer.

*Do I have anything to lose? I mean, I've done this once before already; it's not like I'm starting from scratch. What's the worst that could happen? I go home with one single dollar, and they say they don't want me?*

I paused for a few more minutes.

*I feel like I'm already in hell, might as well dance in the flames.*

"Sure. I'm down," I said.

"Great! So what you're going to want to do is head through the doors and ask one of the bartenders to show you to the dressing room. Tell them Sean sent you and if they give you shit for it, come back here and I'll take care of it. You'll find a drag queen backstage named Celeste Teal, she has the schedule for the boys. Follow the schedule, and my manager will review the security footage of your dancing and call you tomorrow sometime with his decision," he said.

"Ok, sounds good, thanks," I said.

After I sipped the last of my sugary, concentrated beverage, Enrique and I passed through the saloon doors that led into the bar.

"Shut up," I growled at Enrique, who was making a very goofy grin in my peripheral vision.

"Ah! Bitch! You're going to be a dancer here! Holy crap, this is so exciting! Maybe we'll be neighbors," he said. "Maybe they'll start a commission on sexy go-go dancers and you could be one of the ambassadors!"

"Fantastic, at least I'll end up being an ambassador of something," I said as dryly as I possibly could.

Enrique began cackling his famous cackle as I approached the bar and asked a bartender to show me to the dressing room. Enrique brought his lips to my ear.

"Papi is going to go to the ATM, you nail this audition, bitch. I know you will," he whispered before grabbing my left ass cheek and disappearing to the front of the club.

In the thirty seconds it took to get to the dressing room, my mind started to wander off again. After I graduated from undergrad, I took a trip to Chicago with my mom to visit my older brother, Drake, who had just moved there. While taking a night cruise of the city, we learned some fun facts about the Windy City, including many of its famous residents, such as William Wrigley. We learned that Wrigley did not initially sell gum but rather baking powder and other cosmetics. At first, business was terrible, but it didn't stop Wrigley from working tirelessly to perfect his products. After months of changing his product lines, he came up with a genius marketing idea. He decided to lure people into his store by offering them a stick of chewing gum to chew on while they shopped in his store. The logic went that if potential customers were offered a stick of gum to chew on while they shopped, then they'd be more likely to stay longer and buy something. The chewing gum ended up becoming more popular than the cosmetics, and Wrigley had found a new calling.

I knew that I had a set of other skills. Wrigley probably felt the same way about his cosmetic products, which took him months to perfect, but it was not what the market was demanding. Putting these two events together next to each other, I felt like, instead of beating myself up for not selling my cosmetics, maybe I should switch to selling gum instead.

Upon arriving in the dressing room, I had very little preparation to do. I was already in my underwear and dancing shoes. I was told to wait for the drag queen to arrive and go from there. The dressing room was in a basement, where it was eerily quiet. I looked into the mirror and saw myself in the reflection. Ring lights are God's gift to the gays who want to look good. Looking straight ahead into the mirror, I didn't care that I wasn't looking at a suited diplomat; I was looking at an unemployed mess at his wits' end. Coincidentally, I chose to wear the cock ring that evening, you can never go wrong with some silicon support. Time to razzle-dazzle.

Not long after, I heard the clicking and clacking of some very sensible high heels. In my reflection, I saw a glamorous drag queen making her way down the stairs. She had a purse dangling from her left arm and a diet soda clutched firmly in her right hand. As soon as we made eye contact, she let out a loud exclamation.

"Baby! I heard we got some fresh meat up in this bitch," she exclaimed.

"That would be me," I said, faking a cheerful disposition.

"Hey, sweetie, I'm Celeste Teal," she said. "What's yours, baby boy?"

"I'm DJ," I said, kissing the top of her palm. "Pleasure is all mine."

"Oh my, and he's a charmer too," she said, blushing. "Is this your first time dancing, cutie?"

"Not my first time," I said. "I've danced once before, back in my hometown."

*Yeah, and then once again in a fucking creepy zoological dream sequence, if that counts.*

"Lovely, and where exactly is your hometown, gorgeous?" she asked.

"I'm from the Central Valley, close to Yosemite," I said.

*Not close at all, but whatever.*

"Well, welcome, we are so happy to have you here, handsome. So you probably already know how this goes: make sure you look sexy and fun. Make sure your booty hole never sees the light of day, or we'll get our asses shut down. Thrusting is fine just make sure no messy bitches yank your undies down; if they do just make eye contact with the security and they'll take care of it," she said.

I felt relieved again. As disoriented as I was, it felt nice to know that at least two people in that bar had my back.

"Any questions, love?" she asked.

"What kind of dancing should I do to impress the manager?" I asked.

She looked down at my bulge, which was now pushing against my underwear in the ring.

"Baby, with all that going on, just shake it like there's no tomorrow," she said with a wink. "I'm going to go get some shots. The other boys should be here soon. What would you like to drink?"

"I'll take a shot of vodka or whiskey if you've got it," I said.

"You got it, two shots of whiskey coming right up," she said with another wink, which made me smile.

I started doing some stretching, making sure my hamstrings were nice and loose. The pitter-patter of four feet preceded the arrival of the other two dancers, who immediately greeted me with hugs and started stripping. We exchanged small talk for a few minutes, reminding me that most go-go dancers are normal, pleasant people. Celeste came back down a few minutes later with a tray of five shots.

"Alright, boys, come drink with Mama, let's go," she said, passing the shots to each of us. "And one extra one for the sexy auditionee."

Feeling touched, I winked at Celeste as our shot glasses clinked together.

"Cheers, bitches," she said as we all downed our liquor. "Alright, we're going to have the newbie start with you, Tony, up on main, and Benji, you can have side until we do a switch around. Don't worry, newbie, this will all make sense soon. Don't forget to get that oil to look nice and shiny, alright, boo? I've got to go out now, you boys be nice to the newbie; if either of you get bitchy, your bare asses will end up over my knee, okay?"

Tony and Benji started laughing, giving me insight into this little group dynamic at the bar. It reminded me of the playful teasing from both my theater friends and Jordy and the other Fresno dancers. That warm feeling mixed with the alcohol made me temporarily forget to be nervous again before an audition with money on the line. We chatted for a bit longer down in the basement before we heard a loud shouting coming from the staircase.

"Tony, grab the newbie and bring your sexy asses up here now!" Celeste shouted down.

*Fuck. Showtime. Remember, work the bulge. Thrust the bulge. Be the bulge, that's the money maker. At least one of my heads will land me an income.*

We walked up to the club floor, where a few more people had shown up. It was by no means crowded, but looked somewhat decent for a Monday. Tony brought me up to "main," which was short for mainstage, a rectangular platform in the middle of the club. Side, on the other hand, was a single box closer to the bar on the side of the room.

"Just have fun," Tony said as we both started moving to the beat.

This felt a little different than dancing at Flash because back then, I had a little bit of hope left in me. In the months since I was on one of these boxes, my drinking habits had gotten worse, some random friend had called a hotline thinking I was suicidal, I had moved and lived in several different cities, Damien died, my boss took advantage of me, and my car got broken into. Hope in my prospects and just humanity in general were at an all-time low; all I had left was the stage and a resonating beat coming from the sound booth. I began to dance like I had no fucks left to give, because I didn't.

A few people in the crowd were dancing to the beat, but nobody was really on the dance floor. Only a couple of people were actively dancing, but after a while, a few people made their way to the dance floor. I kept grooving back and forth to the beat and looked at the back of the bar. Just like at Flash, nobody was really actively looking at me. Almost everybody was either glued to a smartphone, chatting with friends, or making out with someone. That box I was dancing on began to feel as lonely and unfulfilling as the box in Flash had.

As I shifted my gaze toward the back of the bar, I locked eyes with Enrique, who had been staring at me like I was the only boy in the entire club. True to form, he strutted over to me and folded his arms, sizing me up like he was in an art museum. Knowing what turned him on, I turned around and started shaking my hips rapidly from side to side.

I started shaking my ass near his face so he could tip me. After I reached back to pull the bill out of my waistband, I saw that he had only put a one-dollar bill in my waistband. It was impossible not to bust out into laughter with Enrique; even when I was in a cranky mood, he always knew how to make me laugh. He reached back into his wallet for another bill and pulled it out.

"Don't you fucking dare," I yelled over the music as my eyes widened threateningly.

It was too late. He quickly shoved a big fat Benjamin Franklin right into my waistband, and I knew he wasn't going to take it back, especially given how sweaty I already was. I rolled my eyes at him, to which he responded with a wink before heading to another part of the bar.

*He's just doing this because he feels bad for you. This is going to be the only tip you're going to make tonight. No, maybe everyone will see the $100 and want to tip more.*

I danced for another hour or so. The bar did not get all that much busier, but I received a solid amount of tips, given how few people were there. I was able to dance with both Tony and Benji, who repeatedly shot me winks of encouragement. Suddenly, the box didn't feel as lonely. After I said my goodbyes to the boys and Celeste, I bumped into Sean and thanked him.

"No, thank you! You can expect a call sometime tomorrow from my boss around four. I saw some of your moves, you did great, cutie," he said.

*I really hope that will influence the final decision tomorrow.*

"Thanks," I said as I headed out of the club, hopped in Enrique's car, and headed back to his apartment.


I woke up the next day on the couch feeling dizzy, emotionally, and physically. I had slept on so many different beds in the previous four months, so waking up always began with a question: where the hell am I today? The coffee maker was particularly pungent that morning as Enrique pranced around merrily in the kitchen getting ready for his day. He was always in an annoyingly chipper mood in the morning.

"Good morning, sexy dancer boy," Enrique said.

"I don't even know if they're going to hire me yet, so don't jinx it," I said.

"I'm manifesting good vibes for you, papi," he said. "Did they say when you would know?"

"I'm expecting a phone call at four today," I said.

"Love that! So, I'm only working a half day today in person, so I'll see you at one. Be a good boy and don't burn my house down, ok?"

"Later," I said.

Enrique, in his full business attire, threw on his backpack and waltzed merrily out the door. Watching him walk off dressed so formally while I was still in nothing but my underwear and a five o'clock shadow on the couch was a perfect summation of where we were both at in life. Still feeling numb, I drifted back off to sleep for another couple of hours.

I woke up, stretched for a bit on the floor, and went back to working on my murder mystery play for the theater. It was a good distraction for a couple of hours, but it didn't take long before I reverted to panicking and feeling nervous.

"I'm back! And I brought snacks for you!" Enrique hollered, busting down the door.

*This bitch makes it hard to hate him.*

"I need you to hold my hand," I said.

"Why, what's wrong?" he said. "Oh, wait! That's right!"

*Yeah. That's what's wrong, you fully-employed ass hat.*

It was finally four o'clock, the moment of truth. Five minutes went by, ten minutes went by, and I started panicking.

"They're probably just nervous to call such a sexy boy," Enrique teased, trying to make me feel better.

"Or they forgot about me," I said.

"Yeah, well, they're bitches if they do," he said.

After fifteen minutes, the phone finally rang and I accepted the call. Enrique held my hand the entire time with one hand and rubbed my back with the other. After a few minutes on the line, I hung up.

"Well? Is it a yes?" Enrique asked.

"No," I said, disappointed.

"Oh, so it's a no, then, huh?" he said, mirroring my disappointment.

"No," I said.

"Wait, what? So, it's not a yes or a no?" he asked, perplexed.

"He said the managers thought I was sexy but that I'm not a good enough dancer," I said.

"Well, did they see how much money you made?" he asked.

"Yes, and that's why they're going to give me another chance to audition, but under two conditions. One, I have to do a crash course on go-go dancing with some guy named Javier," I said.

"Oh, that kind of sounds fun! What was the other condition?" he asked.

"I have to dress more like a go-go dancer, like with a harness and everything," I said.

"Sounds like we need to go shopping," he said. "Get dressed."

"Wait, now? Don't you have work?" I asked.

"Hybrid work, baby," he said, jiggling his phone in my face with his signature smirk.

*One of these days, I'm going to slap that smirk off. But in a loving way.*


Enrique drove me to a store in Denver that sold underwear and other queer apparel. Since it was a weekday, the store was practically empty. I approached the employee who was stocking the swimsuit section and politely inquired as to where I could find a fit for go-go dancing. The employee sized me up for a microsecond and then informed me that I was eligible for a 25% "entertainers' discount."

*Well, I guess I look the part, and I'm going to save money. Huzzah.*

I went to the dressing room in the back with a handful of selections. I tried each of them out one by one and, as usual, began feeling very indecisive. I tried on two very tight-fitting jockstraps and a full harness set. Given my budget, I ended up just choosing one of the jockstraps with the harness that I thought would look good.

"Let's see those sexy go-go buns," Enrique said from the other side of the fitting room.

I walked out in a tight neon jockstrap with a blue harness and did a little twirl for Enrique and the store employee.

"Well?" I asked.

"They just grow up so fast," Enrique said, pretending to wipe a tear from his eye.

"Shut up, how does it look?" I said, trying not to laugh.

"I'd hit it," the store employee said, to Enrique's thunderous laughter.

"See!" Enrique squawked.

*He's just saying that because these two pieces are the most expensive of all the outfits. He's also probably horny all day and says that to everyone.*

"Well, I'm only going to buy one outfit, so—" I said.

"Nope, that's where you're wrong. *I'm* going to buy you all of those outfits," Enrique interrupted. "Just as long as you model them all for me."

*This bitch is the real deal. Generous doesn't even come close to it. Maybe I won't slap his smirky face after all.*


I arrived at Chuckie's the following afternoon for my training.

"Hi, I'm supposed to meet with Javier. Do you know where I can find him?" I asked the bartender.

"I haven't seen him yet," the bartender grumbled as he pointed to the smaller, second dance floor in a secluded section of the bar. "But you can wait for him in there."

"Ok," I said, not wanting to inconvenience the grumpy bartender anymore.

I made my way over to the side of the dance floor and began doing some stretches. I had hoped that if Javier saw me doing stretches as he walked in, then he would get the impression that I was deeply serious about working there. During my stretches, I peeked through the clear doors to witness a cast of characters that resembled exactly what you would think would be a group of people who day drink during the week. Of course, I was in no place to judge because that is more than likely what I would be doing at home by myself if I hadn't been given this second chance.

After a long series of stretches, I stared at myself in the large, bedazzled mirror behind the stage. I never counted the number of times that I had looked into the mirror of the past year, expecting to see a suited diplomat or academic looking back at me. By this time, I had looked into enough mirrors to feel like I had completely metamorphosed into a go-go boy.

Javier arrived shortly after. We kissed on both cheeks and then immediately got to work. He went over to the DJ booth and played some warm-up music.

"Actually," he said, interrupting his little sound check. "Let me get you up to speed here."

*Oh god, here comes the roast.*

"I wanted to let you know that we don't do this often, but I saw a lot of potential even though the managers didn't care for your audition," he said.

*Ok. Mixed feedback. This could have been a lot fucking worse. Is he lying to me? Is this a good cop/bad cop routine we're doing here?*

"Oh, ok. Well, just out of curiosity, what did the managers say?" I asked.

"Well, they said you looked very sexy. There were just times when you were dancing a little bit like you wanted to make people laugh," he said.

*Well, excuse the hell out of me for being both sexy and funny!*

"Oh, ok, I see," I responded with a straight face.

"Yeah, there were times when you were doing great moves, but then other times it looked a little bit too cartoony," he said.

*I will make damn sure that Javier and Jordy never end up in the same room together. Ever.*

"Yeah, I like to make people laugh, it's kind of my default state, so thank you for pointing that out to me," I said.

"Well, yeah, being funny is great, but not when you're on a go-go box. You're supposed to be peoples' fantasy, you want to make them horny not laugh," he explained.

*I'm proud to be able to do both, but whatever.*

"Understood," I said.

"Ok. That was the first thing," he said.

*Oh god, there's more.*

"The other thing is," he looked me in the eye uncomfortably. "And please don't take this personally."

*My life is a fucking aimless dumpster fire right now, I give very few fucks about anything anymore. Just say it.*

"You danced a little bit too..." he said, pausing awkwardly.

*Ok, spit it out right now or I'm going to throw up all over this dance floor.*

"White," he said.

"Yeah, I know," I said.

Like most stereotypes, the one regarding European descendants not being able to dance or just generally not having any rhythm at all comes from somewhere. I began to wonder if my silliness both at the audition and at the summer showcase was a deflection to distract from my lack of dancing abilities. Regardless, I was ready to take the criticism with grace and work my ass off to improve and show that I had what it took to be on that box.

"So pick a song that you would want to do a lap dance to," he said.

*Oh god. What the fuck have I gotten myself into.*

I froze. I completely blanked on the name of a song.

*Song, song, songs, I can't think of a song! What was music even? Just say something, stupid.*

"You need to be prepared at all times with a go-to song, so give me a song in the next five seconds or I'm choosing one for you," he said.

"Partition!" I blurted out.

After staring me down for about three seconds, he went over to the DJ booth and played the song. At the beginning of the song, where there is dialogue, Javier placed a chair right in front of the mirror and gestured for me to go over to it.

"Ok, now pretend some rich old dude is sitting here and you're going to convince him to take you home using only your hips," he instructed.

*Ok, I love dancing, but this feels a little strange. Whatever.*

"Alright, got it," I said.

I ruffled up my hair a bit, then began moving my hips from side to side slowly and seductively. Javier came behind me and guided my hips.

"Squat down a bit more, arch your back, and there we go," he said.

*Jesus, I feel like a slutty Eliza Doolittle.*

I kept gyrating around the invisible businessman and tried to maintain a sexy smolder on my face. With all of that movement, worrying about screwing up, I was surprised to hear positive feedback from Javier.

"Yes, there it is! A little more hip movement, Papa," Javier encouraged.

*God, what did my ancestors think when they were on the boat headed to the United States for a better life? Did they think that this is what their descendants would be doing?*

"More movement! Yes! Keep grinding, now go in for the thrust. Damn, papi, that's what I'm talking about!" he said.

*Am I really doing it?*

"You're doing it! Hell yeah, you're all sexy, no silly this time," he said. "Damn, I'm getting a hard on, and I bet that invisible businessman is too!"

We continued practicing for another half an hour or so. He taught me a few other moves, and then we wrapped up.

"You have a lot of potential, papi. Like I said, we don't normally do this for boys, but I think you can do it if you practice," Javier said after hugging me goodbye. "See you next week."

"Thanks for everything, I won't let you down," I said.

If you recall, 2023 was the summer of "Barbenheimer," a release of two blockbuster films: *Barbie*, a bubble gum pop flick about a doll, and *Oppenheimer*, a historical epic about the creation of the atom bomb. That summer, moviegoers of all types dressed up for both occasions, with bright pink outfits for *Barbie* and dark, sinister ones for *Oppenheimer*.

Enrique and I went to *Oppenheimer* the first night. Being history buffs, we enjoyed the three-hour epic and the conversations that it stimulated about power, greed, genocide, secrecy, and unintended consequences. We spent hours at another Thai place afterwards discussing the movie, the Cold War, and the different outfits we had seen moviegoers in that day.

I woke up the next morning feeling empty, as usual. Enrique woke up feeling chipper, as usual.

"Morning, sexy! So, bad news, I don't think I'm going to make it to see Barbie with you today," Enrique said sheepishly. "They pushed back both of my meetings so I won't be able to dip out of work early."

"I thought you were hybrid," I said, mimicking the same gesture with my phone that Enrique had done the day before.

"You bitch!" he said laughing. "You'll have to tell me all about it. Hope the world doesn't blow up in this one."

"It probably won't, which is kind of a pity," I said dryly.

"Well, have fun, and I'll see you later tonight. Are we doing underwear night at Tavern?" he said.

"Yeah, I'm down," I said.

"Cool, be a good boy and I'll see you later, sexy," he said.

"Sounds good, enjoy work," I said as Enrique exited the apartment.

It was early afternoon when I arrived at the theater. To fit in with the Barbie theme, I wore a bright pink polo even though I had Oppenheimer written all over my droopy, depressed face. As the movie started, the audience and I were bombarded with so much pink, joy, and fun. Girls and gays made up, I'd say, 90% of the theater, and the other 10% were presumably straight boyfriends. Regardless of demographic, almost everyone seemed to be laughing and having a good time the whole movie, but not me. I was dazzled by the colors and the performances, but I was having a hard time enjoying the parts of the film that were meant to make the audience happy. It felt like Times Square all over again: bright, colorful lights felt gray and unappealing. Joy and laughter could not warm my hardened heart; I was wholly unprepared to be impacted so heavily by the ending.

In one of the final scenes, Margot Robbie's Barbie meets the ghost of Ruth Handler, the creator of Barbie and founder of Mattel, set against the backdrop of a song written by Billie Eilish. The melancholy song is about feeling empty, unfulfilled, and only wanted for one's exterior.

*What the fuck is happening? Why am I crying? Stop crying.*

Tears began to slowly rush down my face as Ruth Handler held Barbie's hands and instructed her to feel. That simple word "feel" sent me from a moderate cry into a severe sob. I put my face in my hands and cried harder than I had in a long time. For the previous year or so, I had cried many times, but this was much different. The culmination of both non-stop rejection, not being heard or understood, disillusionment in humanity, and feeling like an empty object was all bundled into a single song that struck a chord with me like no other song had before. For the past year, I had received positive feedback for my exterior self, but, as the film suggests, that exterior is temporary and leaves one feeling empty.

When everyone exited the theater, most people were laughing, humming some of the happier songs from the film, and chatting about how great it was. Then there was me, a big sobbing mess, unable to hold back tears. I burst out of the theater and began to hyperventilate.

*Breathe, breathe. It's ok, the movie is over. Focus on breathing, don't stop breathing.*

I squatted over my knees in a sort of fetal position as I continued to sob and began to feel nauseous.

*I don't have my inhaler. This is the worst possible fucking time to not have my inhaler, shit!*

I called Enrique, but the call went to voicemail. I called Gavin, but the call went to voicemail as well. I kept calling back and forth, but kept being sent to voicemail.

After staying in that position for what felt like an eternity, Enrique called me back.

"Hey, Barbie boy, is everything ok?" he asked.

The outburst of sounds I made was enough of an answer for him.

"Do you need me to come pick you up?" he asked.

I continued to cry into the phone before I could make out an intelligible response.

"No, I just need—I just need a minute," I said.

Enrique stayed mostly silent on the other end of the line as I let out gasps and tried to get my breathing under control.

"Ok, fuck. Ok, no, I'm sorry. I'm good now. I think I can drive," I said, still recovering.

"Are you sure?" he asked.

"Yes, see you soon," I said.

Driving through downtown Denver helped calm me down. The sun vanished behind the Rocky Mountains as the sky turned bright purple. I rolled down the window and stuck my hand out to feel the warm summer breeze flow through my fingers as I got my breath under control.

Enrique was waiting for me with a big hug when I got back to his apartment. Freshly popped popcorn awaited me on the couch, next to a box of tissues. He held my hand with one hand and rubbed my back with the other.

"And this all started because of that song?" Enrique asked.

"Well, the song just kind of summarized every shitty feeling in a very succinct way, and the tone and rhythm just struck a chord," I said.

"How so?" he asked.

"Just that line about just being something paid for, that's just what I feel like. I'm having a hard time feeling anything more than a doll now. I get attention, which is fun. Yes, I get played with, which is fun. But, as you'll see when you watch the movie, what happens to Barbie dolls? Eventually, they get thrown out as soon as their usefulness wears off. I felt that way working on the campaigns, we talked to all these people and then as soon as the election was over, we never spoke to them again, their usefulness to us went away," I said.

"Well, I'm going to have to push back on that a little bit because *I* still did quite a bit of that after the election," he said.

"Sure, you're a glorious exception, but that's what the world is, just take, take, take, and then leave for dead. The press keeps talking about Barbenheimer like the movies are different, but they really aren't. Oppenheimer was useful when he designed the bomb, and then he was just discarded, and Barbie was useful and then she was discarded," I said.

"And this is news to you, Mr. Mayberry?" he asked with a little smirk.

"What do you mean?" I asked.

"Did no one tell you that life was going to be this way?" he sang before quickly clapping four times.

*I hate it when I'm trying to be serious and sad and this bitch makes me laugh.*

As much as I tried fighting it, I couldn't help but let out a chuckle.

"Well, that song made you sad, but this song should make you feel better," he said, singing the rest of the *Friends* theme song.

*How could something so stupidly corny make me cry again?*

"Go to hell," I snapped back through tears and bated chuckles.

"Only if you get to bunk with me, but I call dibs on the bottom bunk," he said.

"That's where you belong, boy," I said in a cartoonishly deep cowboy voice as I pinched his left butt cheek.

"Ouch! So sexy! Well I love you and I want you to know that I will love you if you end up as a sexy go-go dancer, a diplomat, a hooker, a professor, or any combination of those things," he said.

"Maybe I'll be all four of those things at once, just imagine what my resume would look like," I joked.

*I was sobbing just a few hours ago, and now he's gotten me back to cracking jokes. He really does bring out the best in me. I hate him for that.*

We started watching TV and chatting about Enrique's day at work. It seemed horrible and made me feel even more grateful to leave behind the prospects of working in politics. After a few minutes of chomping on the popcorn, my phone rang again. It was Gavin.

"Hey, sorry, I think I butt-dialed you earlier," I lied.

I didn't want to explain my emotional meltdown over the phone.

"No, it's ok, I was meaning to call you anyway," Gavin said. "I don't have a whole lot of time now, but I'm at dinner with an old friend of mine who works at the community college here, and I think I have a job for you if you're interested."

*Oh god, here we go again.*

"You'd be tutoring ESL students in the non-credit program. You're more than qualified for it," he said. "There are two catches, though: it starts next Monday, and it's only temporary until they find a permanent person. If you want to apply for it, you'll have to be interviewed with other candidates. Are you down?"

"Well," I paused, looking at Enrique.

*Well, you could take the chance of being a sexy dancer here and keep descending into despair, or you could go back home, make some money, and heal. Is this really even a debate?*

"It's yours if you want it, I just need to know now so I can tell my friend," he said.

"Yes, I'm in," I said. "See you Monday."

I hung up the phone. Enrique had clearly been eavesdropping.

"Well, we've got professor checked off the list, only three more professions to go," he joked. "Get your undies on, bitch. Let's go celebrate."

Feeling relieved by not only a new job opportunity but also time to heal, I went to the underwear night at the club feeling cautiously optimistic. All it took was one phone call and suddenly the song from *Barbie* didn't sting as much.

Enrique and I did some loops around the bar. We visited with some friends we had known and made some new friends too. Towards the end of the night, I bumped into Jake, a friend I had met on a previous trip to Denver. When we met, we were both depressed and would drink a lot together and commiserate over our respective situations: he was hating his job, and I was lamenting not having a job. The camaraderie felt nice, but eventually devolved into us drinking more when we were together, either virtually or in person, and not fixing our problems.

We proceeded to have that same conversation, but since I had just received a job offer to work at a community college, I did more listening. He was ranting about how miserable he was and how much anger he felt towards himself and where he was in life. As the conversation went on, I disassociated briefly and had another epiphany.

*This is going to be you if you don't change course now. You have a choice. Keep drinking your problems away, or face them like a man.*

My heart began pounding again, and words flowed out of my mouth before my brain had time to stop them.

"Jake, I need to tell you something: I love you. I really fucking love you, but I'm going to be honest. When I get back home, I'm going to stop drinking my problems away. I love you, but I really hope you do too," I said.

Taken aback, he paused for a moment. I stared into his eyes and began to see tears form in the corners. Still drunk, his chin began to quiver.

He nuzzled his face into my neck and began to sob as intensely as I had after watching *Barbie*. I began to rub his back just as Enrique had done to me so many times before. The tears were dripping down my neck and onto my collarbone.

Enrique walked up to me and began tapping his wrist, indicating that it was time to go. He was my ride, and I had a long day of traveling ahead of me. It was time to say goodbye to Jake.

"I love you, and I hope you take care of yourself," I said, helping wipe his tears.

We hugged one more time, then parted ways. I followed Enrique back to the car. The car ride was rather silent, and I began thinking about the two friends I had just spent a lot of time with in the bar. On the one hand, Enrique had been sober at that point for about eight years and had completely turned his life around. Jake, on the other hand, was also employed but was essentially a functioning alcoholic.

Just as I had experienced after Mexico when Damien died, I was facing a fork in the road. This temporary job offer I received presented me with the opportunity to build a foundation to rebuild my life. I had seen enough and had battled my own demons to know which road to take.

The next morning, Enrique's coffee machine woke me up again. After sharing a lovely breakfast, we headed down to the parking garage to get into our cars and go our separate ways.

"Drive safe, tell me how your mystery play goes down. Oh, and give my best to your mommy for me," he said.

I gave him a massive hug, got into my car, and began to head west.

As I left Denver, I called my mom and told her (most) of what had happened the previous two months. She sounded relieved and happy that I was returning home to heal and rebuild my life. I also called Javier to let him know that the second audition wasn't going to happen.

After I hung up the phone, it started to sprinkle. An eclectic combination of dark clouds, light clouds, and clear blue sky loomed over the majestic snowcapped Rocky Mountains as the rain intensified. I played "What Was I Made For" and continued to reflect as I watched the view in front of me fully encapsulate life at that moment: a kaleidoscope of dark and light clouds, sunlight in the distance, and rain pouring down at full intensity in one moment and at other times stopping completely. But at least there was light somewhere.

# CHAPTER 8

## LA LA LAND

Upon my return to California, my unpredictable year continued to be unpredictable.

The Monday after I returned, I started onboarding at my new job. I went through all the trainings, completed all the paperwork, and got off to a wonderful start. My working hours were later in the afternoon, a boon for a night owl like myself. After a while, a stable routine began to take shape: wake up in the late morning, practice Chinese and/or Spanish, go to the gym for a couple of hours, tan outside, take a nap, and then go to work. After work, my parents and I would snack on popcorn and watch a movie together, usually a documentary. We'd play a few hands of cards, chomp on some chips and salsa, and then head to bed. The routine became mundane, but it was a welcome break from the unpredictability and seemingly endless chaos.

The job itself was a complete breath of fresh air. The students I taught were learning English at various levels, but each of them was learning English for different reasons. One particular student from Ukraine had moved to the U.S. with her daughter and had aspirations of becoming a nurse. A large group of my students from Mexico was older and wanted to learn English simply to communicate with their grandchildren. As a fifth-generation American, the concept of not being able to speak intergenerationally with my parents or grandparents was a foreign concept. Being able to eavesdrop on their conversations taught me a lot, brought me down to earth, and made me leave work feeling like I was making a positive difference in people's lives.

The job being part-time granted me a lot of time to relax, rejuvenate, exercise more intensely, and reflect on the year, particularly the summer from hell. After a few weeks and a brief bout with COVID, I started branching out a little more and regained my status as a social butterfly. I ventured up to Fresno more often and made some new friends who enjoyed both clubbing and doing nerdy things. Going out felt exciting again and not like a chore, just to get me out of bed.

With the job, my newfound friends, and extra time to relax, I began to slowly rebuild my self-confidence. To be clear, I was not fully recovered; some damage just simply can't be undone. But for what it was worth, I enjoyed and appreciated having the basics: a steady paycheck, a comfortable home, and a small but very supportive friend group.

As Gavin had mentioned, the job I had taken was temporary, and I had to apply for the position with all the other applicants. Unfortunately, when the time came to hire someone permanently, the college went with another candidate. This was very discouraging because I was beginning to establish a good relationship and rapport with my students. Disappointed though I was, it truly ended up being a blessing in disguise.

As I sat at the table with my parents for dinner one night after I got the news that I would no longer be working at the community college, my life and my fortunes shifted yet again. This time, it was for the better.

"So, your brother just accepted a new job today," my mom said.

"Oh, that's cool," I said, unfazed.

My brother had also been nomadic around the same time I was, so I hadn't kept close tabs on him as I had in the past. We knew more or less how the other was doing, kind of through a combination of word of mouth, occasional texts, and social media posts.

"Well, the job is in L.A. Your dad and I have been talking, and we have an idea if you are interested," she said.

"I'm listening," I said curiously.

"We think that you're not going to find your dream job in Visalia, you're just not. Drake is considering getting a two-bedroom apartment down in L.A., and we would help you get started, and you can spend some time making connections, networking, and trying to find a job down there. You're probably going to have more opportunities in L.A. than you will here," she said.

"You've got a lot of skills, kid. It's time for people to finally see them," my dad said proudly.

*I can think of a few bar patrons in Fresno and Denver who have seen some of those skills.*

"Does that sound like a good plan?" my mom asked.

"Does that mean I have to live with Rufus and Otis, too?" I said, referring to my older brother's very adorable but obnoxiously loud miniature schnauzers.

"Yes, and you'll probably have to take them out for walks and watch them when he's out of town on business," she said. "But it'll sure beat living with your boomer parents, don't you think?"

"Come on. It hasn't been that bad," I replied.

My mother made a face.

"Yeah, you have a point," I said.

"He has to make a decision soon, so, no pressure, but also you'll need to decide by tomorrow," my mom said.

*Tomorrow? Are you crazy, woman? My mom always does this to me: don't panic, but also there's a giant tarantula on your face right now. No pressure.*

"Ok, I'm in," I said almost immediately.

I didn't even need to think. My parents were right about the job prospects, and I needed a fresh start in a new city.

Later that night, as I was scrolling through old photos, I realized that I had never lived in the same city longer than two years since I graduated from high school.

That's when I had another epiphany: perhaps the reason why I felt so disconnected from everything was because I had been journeying all around the world for so long, searching for connection. The joy I felt from the bonds of friendship at Friendsgiving, for example, came from years and years of nurturing those relationships. After high school, I just seemed to be bouncing around the world in search of something.

*Was I running toward something? Or running from something? Another cliché.*

Either way, it didn't matter. The plan was set for us to move to L.A. the second week of November. I began applying for jobs online again like there was no tomorrow. To my utter shock, I received an offer almost the next day for another job teaching ESL.

*Oh, so now the punk-ass internet job aggregators finally yield me some kind of result.*

Even more miraculous, the institute I would be teaching at seemed eager to have me start as soon as possible. It was only part-time, but I would have about a week between moving in and starting the job to find some other kind of side hustle: bartending, go-go dancing, whatever it took. I'd had a taste of stability when I moved back home from Denver, but I knew that I needed to do more to support myself. The reinvigoration of my life would continue in L.A.


One of the last things I did before I moved to L.A. was schedule an appointment with my therapist. Rita was, and still is, a very warm and personable therapist who had seen me before the pandemic, during the pandemic, and a couple of times during my spiraling phase. I was looking forward to showing her how positive a change the previous couple of months had been.

Arriving at her office a few minutes before the session, I sat down in the lobby, feeling a sense of relief. Rays of sunshine aptly shone into the room and set the mood. Unlike the last time she saw me virtually, I was now showered, shaved, employed, not hungover, and not only able to see the light at the end of the tunnel but so close to basking in it.

*You're doing great. The nightmare is over. Now it's just time to continue picking up the pieces and rebuild.*

Bursting open the door enthusiastically was Rita, stretching out her arms to hug me.

"Hello, hello, handsome boy!" she said enthusiastically. "Gosh, I keep forgetting how tall you are!"

"Well, I keep forgetting how short you are, so right back at you," I teased.

She pretended to be insulted, but I knew she appreciated that my sense of humor was back. This time, when I was joking, it wasn't the kind of dark humor I often deployed as a coping mechanism.

We went into her office, and I made myself comfortable on her couch, eyeing the tissues on the coffee table in case I needed to have a moment. After making a little small talk, we got down to business.

"So, you've had quite a year, haven't you?" she asked.

"A year and a half, if you don't include my blissfully ignorant trip to Europe," I said.

"Yes. We can tackle as many issues as we can in this session. What would you like to talk about, my dear?" she asked.

*Ok, no problem. Let me just get this huge fat ass file out of my filing cabinet.*

"Well, I guess I don't even know where to start," I said.

That was not me being dramatic, I really didn't know where to start.

"Well, first, I need to hear about your murder mystery play!" she said enthusiastically.

"Oh, it could not have gone better. I had a lot of fun writing it. The writing distracted me from a lot of the bullshit; it gave me drive when I didn't have a functioning motor. What's more, our lead actor got COVID the final weekend, so I actually got to perform in the show for two performances," I said.

"That's fantastic!" she said.

"Yeah! I had 24 hours' notice, but everyone came together for an emergency rehearsal. It was a lot to handle, but it all panned out, and we sold out that weekend! Being on stage again with people I love and getting to hang out with old friends was not on my bingo card, but I'm so grateful that it was," I said cheerfully.

"I'm so proud of you," she said.

I smiled back, and then there was a brief pause.

"Do you want to talk about Mississippi?" she asked solemnly.

I paused. I think because the heartache and despair of the previous year had all blended into one giant, ugly blob, it was hard to separate one psychologically damaging crisis from another. It's like when you step on ten Legos, it feels no different than if you step on just three or four.

"Someday, I think I do. For now, I guess I just want to find a thread or a theme that I've been feeling through all of this. Maybe we don't tackle a specific issue, but find a common denominator," I said.

"Ok, well, what have you been feeling in each of these episodes of the shitshow," she asked.

"Well, when you're raised by parents who resemble Ward and June Cleaver, you grow up thinking that most people in the world are good people. You're taught to think that most people in the world behave like the people you grew up with, that there are only a few bad apples, and that as long as you work hard and don't get into too much trouble, you can succeed and live a happy life. I think after I graduated last June, I was still naïve enough to believe that, so when the rejection letters began piling up, it kind of threw my worldview into question. It really sent me further down the rabbit hole when my unpaid campaign work didn't land me a job. Even when I had so many solid and supportive people in my corner, it didn't land me a job. Hard work wasn't paying off, and it certainly didn't matter how polite or pleasant I was. I came to the realization that the world is less like Mayberry and more like Zombieland or Lord of the Flies. It got to the point where I started to think that maybe I was the problem, which got me to start taking it out on myself by drowning out the negative thoughts with liquor. As I started to spiral, I took people who were in my corner for granted. All I cared about was impressing strangers: recruiters, potential employers, hookups, etc. I thought maybe if I proved to those kinds of people that I was good enough to be hired, then maybe the emptiness that was eating away at me would be fulfilled, and I would start feeling better about myself. It became pretty clear that I was just chasing an endless rainbow; the more I tried to chase that fulfillment and acceptance, the more I felt like I was losing it, which made the vicious cycle even more vicious. I had people rooting for me the entire time, and yet I just brushed them aside as an afterthought. Then, when I got into dancing, I went into the same toxic cycle of trying to impress people I barely knew: the promoters, the other dancers, the bar patrons, etc. In a sweat-infused night club where everyone was packed in like sardines and carelessly staring out into space, I spent all of my time chasing that rainbow to nowhere. No one was looking at me, hardly anyone was tipping me, and I felt completely alone, even though the room was packed to full capacity. That was the greatest irony of all: even when I was almost fully exposed, I still did not feel seen. But then—fuck, then there was Damien. When our eyes locked that night at Flash, I knew there was at least one person in that bar not just looking at me but seeing me. That proud smirk he had on his face, all this time I thought that look was him trying to convey that he was proud of me for being up on that box. After all, he was the first one to suggest to me that I give go-go dancing a shot, so I thought 'the look' was him playfully boasting that he felt vindicated in his encouragement. It took me almost a year to realize that what he was really communicating to me was that he was never going to leave me. I think he wanted me to know that he would always be with me, whether it was in the club, at Gavin's house, or...well, now, in spirit. Looking back on it, I don't know why I was so hard on myself that night and so bound and determined to get these random people to like me when such a beautiful soul was there, beaming at me the whole time. The same damn thing happened after I left Mississippi for Denver and ended up again in a nightclub searching desperately for affirmation and love. It was not crowded at all, but, of course, Enrique was there cheering me on and tipping me a ridiculous amount of money. Why was I so desperate for those promoters, other go-go boys, or choreographers to like me when I had Enrique there the whole time? I felt so alone then and, frankly, in all of those shitty situations when I absolutely wasn't. I felt alone at home in Visalia, but I wasn't; I had cousins Facetiming me and parents holding me while I sobbed. I felt empty and alone in Palm Springs, but I wasn't; I had Will, Brad, Mario, Serena, Lauren, and Michelle all checking in on me regularly. I felt angry and alone in New York, but I wasn't; I had Diego and Gabriel going out of their way to show me a good time. I felt lost and alone in Mexico after Damien died, but I wasn't; Charles was there holding my hand all day and through the night. I felt desperate and alone in Mississippi, but I wasn't, I had practically a complete stranger, Darnell, going so far to protect me that he gave me a fucking knife and offered to beat the hell out of that sack of shit who took advantage of me when I was at my lowest. Sure, alcohol might always be there for you, but alcohol also won't check in on you, drive several hours to watch you perform, or make you feel like you belong. And these examples are just close friends and family, I haven't even mentioned Jordy, the lady bikers in Mexico who danced with me, the fabulous drag queens who gave me supportive pep talks and ego boosts, or that anonymous friend who called the suicide hotline when I was headed towards the point of no return. It wasn't until Damien died that I realized some people who are always in your corner could be gone in an instant and shouldn't be taken for granted, ever. The truth is, it was Damien who I should have been dancing for the whole time. Or Enrique. Or Gavin. Or, insert any other friend or family member who loved me during times when I was very unlovable—"

Rita had been staring at me with her signature "time out" hand gesture she reserved for when I would rant too long during a session.

"So, this is great, you're doing great, and I think you're scratching the surface of your thread right there," she said. "Now, boil down exactly what you just said in a few sentences or less, if you can."

Pausing for a moment, the wheels in my head began turning. I finally strung all of those thoughts and memories together and began forming some coherent sentences.

"I should surround myself with the kinds of people who give me 'the look.' I need to be prioritizing and spending my time with the kind of people who will cry with me on the kitchen floor, hold onto them, and never let go. Because people in my life aren't different from people in the club: there are so many of them, but most of them will come and go. There are only a handful of people who will stare at me from beyond the dance floor when nobody else is. That handful of people are worth more than platinum," I said.

"I know you've got more, keep going," she instructed.

"Periods of darkness are inevitable; enduring them alone is not," I said.

"Good. Now say it the DJ way," she said.

I paused one more time.

"When life gives you hell, find people to dance with you in the flames," I said.

"Perfect, that's your new mantra. Now, do you think you can apply that to your day-to-day life?" she asked.

"Sure. In many ways, I think I already have," I said.

"Spill," she said while picking up her cup of tea.

"Well, that temporary job I came out here for decided not to keep me on permanently," I said.

"What? Seriously? Didn't you drive from Denver to Visalia in like a day?" she asked.

"Yes. 16 straight hours in the car," I said.

"I'm sorry. That's poopy," she said.

"Well, yes. But back to applying this concept, they were very gracious to offer me the position in the first place. Had I not gotten that job, brief as it was, I would not have had the foundation to rebuild and rejuvenate. I know jobs will come and go, employers need certain workers, and then all of a sudden, they don't. I could be someone's hot commodity one day, and one day I'm chopped liver, regardless of how hard I work or how much effort I put in. But that's all I am to employers, I'm just another employee. You see it every day, employees who have worked the same job at the same company for over fifty years get a freaking pizza party and a cheap card when they retire. My profession, whether it's go-go dancing or teaching, won't always give me value, but the people who are dancing with me in the flames will," I said.

Rita began writing things down. For the first time in a long while, I didn't feel nervous when Rita started writing down things that I was saying. She nodded her head several times and muttered "good" under her breath as she jotted down notes.

"Like, I know that the college is grateful for what I did; they even threw me a little going-away party. But I didn't feel anywhere near as upset as I thought I would be," I said.

"And why do you think that is?" she asked.

"Because as soon as that party was over, I clocked out and drove up to Fresno to go to underwear night at the club with my new friends up there," I said. "That little group of friends I've made since I've been back have all been super supportive. I mean, a couple of them are little shits but they make me feel supported and cared for. And then there are my theater friends from back home who always have my back. My friend Lauren, the one I told you about who just had a baby, even refers to me as Uncle DJ. Theater friends aren't just friends, they're family."

"Uncle DJ, that's sweet!" she said.

"Yeah, I feel like now I've got a good enough sense to know who's a come-and-go kind of person in my life and who is the kind of person who would both cry with me on the kitchen floor or cheer for me on the dance floor," I said.

"I have to say, that's very beautiful. I'm so proud of you, handsome. You look great and you sound great, I'm excited for you," she said. "Are you? Are you proud and excited for you, too?"

"Yes, I am," I said, with a smile.

"How do you feel about this move to L.A.?" she asked.

"Good. I don't know what to expect. I miraculously got a job teaching English part-time at an institute not too far from our apartment," I said. "And I know that L.A. has a reputation for toxic bitches, but I've lived in enough places to know that toxic bitches are everywhere. At least now I have a better sense of how to pilfer the toxic bitches from the cool bitches now. I feel like I'm Leave it to Beaver wielding a machine gun headed towards Zombieland."

"I'm so excited for you, honey. You're going to be just fine," she said.

"I think so too," I said.

"Well, you know where to reach me. I'm always available for virtual sessions if you don't want to make the long journey back here," she said.

"Thank you so much. For everything," I said, getting up to hug her.


When I woke up the next day, I felt the opposite of what I had felt when I woke up from my naps in Palm Springs, New York, Mexico, Mississippi, and Denver. Instead of waking up to a nightmare, I was waking up to a dream, only it was real. I was ready to start over and have the opportunity to live in one of the biggest, most vibrant cities in the world. I had no idea what was ahead of me, but, unlike my previous journeys, this felt like an exciting new start.

My dad helped my brother and me load our belongings into the moving truck and both of our cars. My brother's doggies popped their final squat before the long drive down south. The three of us hugged my mom goodbye and made our way out. I went back for another hug because my mom gave me more love than I ever deserved during a time when I felt most undeserving of it.

The weather when we arrived on that November afternoon was customary for L.A.: calm, temperate, and warm. We drove down Highway 101 and turned off at Cahuenga. I was so blissful that I was completely unfazed by the potholes, litter, rows of tents, or graffiti lining the underpass.

We made it to the apartment and began unloading our stuff. The three of us kept going up and down the elevators with suitcases, bags, and boxes. After we had unloaded all our stuff, I noticed my dad was not feeling well. His joints are not what they used to be, and the quantity and size of the stuff we had to unload were visibly taking a toll on him. What's more, he had spent a little over a year overcoming his own demons and mental health struggles. And yet, when all the boxes were in our apartment, he looked at me directly.

"What do you need next?" he asked.

My dad. Even when he was fighting through arthritis, he was still as eager as could be to provide us with what we needed. I love that man.

"I have to leave for work soon," my brother said.

"Really, at this hour?" my dad asked.

"Yeah, I've got to be at a happy hour downtown in 15 minutes," he said.

I gave my brother, who is bisexual, a look, subliminally asking him if there was indeed a business-related happy hour or if this was a "happy" hour he was heading off to. His glare and eye roll back at me signaled that it was the former.

After we all said our goodbyes, I got ready to go out and start looking for side hustles. Since I had done plenty of reflecting in Rita's office already, I wasted no time getting a head start in my new city. I got into my dusty old car and immediately met bumper-to-bumper traffic on Santa Monica Boulevard.

*Get used to this, buddy.*

Driving slowly but merrily past the large intersections, I entered the city of West Hollywood. Having done a little research beforehand, I made a little detour to the famous bright pink wall. Picture time! After spending what felt like forever trying to find a parking spot that was accessible, affordable, didn't require a permit, and not in the emergency zone, I headed over to the picturesque Paul Smith wall, a giant pink wall on the building's west and south-facing sides. There were tons of tourists lined up to take photos, which made me giddy.

*I'll be patient. Most of these people look like tourists. I get to live here. Yay!*

Befriending the couple in front of me, we did the classic "tourist photographer swap" where I took their picture and they took mine. Posing for mine with a big thumbs up, I felt like I was officially an Angeleno.

Once I had my first documented couple of photos in my new city, I arrived at the large parking structure in the West Hollywood Park. I slipped the tiny parking pass out of the machine and spiraled up the tall parking structure, finally reaching a parking spot on the third floor. Now that I had been a tourist, it was time to be a businessman. As such, I lowered my tank top as low as I possibly could and lifted my short shorts to show off more of my legs.

*Yes, you look like a businessman.*

I walked through the vast park that included an outdoor gym, a basketball court, both a small and a big dog park, and plenty of bright green grass stretching far and wide. Parents played with their children in the park, musicians plucked away at their guitars, homeless people searched through the trash bins for recyclable cans, and dogs chased after spiraling tennis balls.

From what I had read online, the majority of the clubs were on Santa Monica Boulevard. I made my way up Robertson Avenue and popped into every single one of the bars I could find. The pitch was always the same.

"Hi! My name is DJ. I just moved here, and the job I have is only part-time during the week, but I would love to work here on the weekends. Do you have any jobs available?"

Most bars, to my dismay, were not actively hiring. A few mentioned that they might be hiring closer to the holidays in December, but none were guaranteed. Fortunately, just about every single one of the employees I talked to was very helpful and polite. This was not the L.A. I had envisioned it in my head.

The sun descended, and the famous rainbow orb lights that dangled above Santa Monica Boulevard began to illuminate. I ran back to my car to head home for the evening, but it was still early in the night. I had a lot of time to spare, but I didn't know anybody.

*Just go home, it's been a long day. Tap out, no one will blame you. No! Seize the day! Go and make friends, this will be fun for you! The internet will give you nothing but shallow one-off meetings that won't go anywhere. Go into the wild and be yourself; you might be surprised by what happens. You've got nothing to lose and everything to gain. But it's so damn cold! And I didn't bring my, wait, aww, fuck, I do have a sweatshirt. There goes that excuse. Ok, fine. I'll do it. Happy now?*

I slid my sweatshirt on, locked my car, and headed back to the bars. It felt like there were twice as many people out and about as when I left. I started walking towards the bars and paused outside of one of them called "Bye Bottoms." This particular bar had multiple tables outside and was starting to draw a crowd. While scanning the bar from outside, I noticed one particular group of guys occupying a large table on the right side of the bar. They varied in both age and appearance, not what I would have expected from a gaggle of gays in West Hollywood.

In a manner of confidence that matched the beginning of my safari nightmare in Palm Springs, I walked up to the group of guys. Awkwardly standing in the middle of the rectangular table, I paused until the conversation ended.

*Make a good first impression, don't blow it.*

"Hi, I'm DJ, I'm new to town. You want to be friends?" I asked, bluntly.

Most guys at the table were initially stunned and then began to chuckle at how brazen I was. After an awkward pause, the group surprisingly all welcomed me one by one. Making my rounds, I shook hands with everyone in the group. The last member of the group whose hand I shook was a beefier guy wearing a purple turtle neck sweater and a golf cap at the edge of the table.

"I'm DJ," I said.

"I'm Terry," said the man as he shook my hand warmly.

"Yes, you are," I said, flirting a little bit with my eyes.

"And, you're DJ? What's DJ short for?" he asked.

"Can you guess?" I asked.

"I'm better at guessing dick sizes than abbreviations, actually," he said.

*Match made in heaven, he is as brazen as you are!*

"And what is Terry short for?" I joked back.

"It's short for I think I need to buy you a drink, newbie," he quipped back, not even skipping a beat.

Wow. That was fast. In less than two minutes, I introduced myself to at least ten potential new friends, and now it was time to enjoy a drink.

*It's because you're a dirty slut. Ok, yes but a dirty slut who needs to unwind. Bring on the cocktails!*

"What would you like, handsome boy?" Terry asked.

"A Dirty Shirley," I said back.

Terry shot a look back at me with a twinge of judgment.

"Did you just turn 21? Are you in a sorority?" he asked sarcastically.

"No, but I could be in a frat. I do have a paddle," I said with a wink.

"Oh my god," he said, laughing. "Come with me."

I followed Terry to the bar. He seemed to know everybody, or at least everybody knew him. We bumped into five or six different people who said hello to him before we eventually made it to the bar. In less than five minutes of knowing him, I would learn that Terry had been dubbed the unofficial mayor of West Hollywood.

"So, if you're the unofficial mayor, can I be the people's princess?" I asked.

"What are you talking about?" Terry said with a chuckle.

"Oh, I kind of have this obsession with Princess Diana. I want to help people in need but also get revenge on my haters by looking hot as fuck in black," I explained. "It's weird because I never knew Diana when she was popular, though; my knowledge of her is all from documentaries and movies. She died when I was two."

Hitting some kind of nerve with Terry, he shoved his face into his hands.

"Oh my god, shut up. You are like an embryo," he said.

"No, I'm not. I remember where I was during Hurricane Katrina," I said.

"Ok, but do you remember where you were during the Bronco chase?" he said, referring to O.J. Simpson's infamous low-speed chase up the 405 freeway.

"Sure, I do. Half of me was in my father and the other half was in my mother," I joked.

"Oh my god, you're such a goofball. You'll fit in well with our group," he said.

We made it back to the table for a lightning round of questions: where I was from, where I went to school, what I studied, where I moved to, etc. Then the topic of what I did for work came up, which immediately got the attention of the entire table. Getting a gaggle of gays to put their phones down and pay attention for even five seconds is a goddamn miracle.

"Wait, a go-go dancer? Do we have a go-go dancer friend now?" one of Terry's friends said.

*Friend? Already? Do they see me as a friend? Come on, they don't even know me. I could be a serial killer for all they know. Now that I think about it, I could have been such a successful sociopath if my parents hadn't raised me to have a conscience.*

"Wait, are you seriously a go-go dancer?" Terry asked.

"Well, I've only done it a couple of times before, so I'm not super experienced. Like, I can't twerk or use the pole or anything like that, but a paycheck is a paycheck, and I'll go wherever or do whatever I need to do to make ends meet here. My part-time job only covers some of my bills, so this would help me get by," I said.

Terry looked at me straight in the eye. This look did not feel too dissimilar to the look that Damien had given me in Gavin's backyard nearly a year prior; he didn't even blink.

"Hey Dylan, is Carlos going to be at Sanctuary tonight?" Terry asked, maintaining his gaze on me.

"Uh, he's supposed to be, let me text him," Dylan said.

"Thanks, Dylan, um, I'm sorry, but what's Sanctuary?" I said.

The entire table paused and stared at me with pure shock and judgment. They all looked at me like I was from another planet. Our community can be so judgmental. Gays might not disown you, but they will always make their opinions very much known.

"Ok, she's new in town, be nice girls," Terry scolded. "The Sanctuary is a popular gay bar here that has go-go dancers almost every night. We're heading over there in a few for their musical theater night. Our buddy Carlos is a go-go dancer there, we can introduce you."

*Did I hear that right? Musical theater night?*

"Yup, he said he's on tonight," Dylan said.

"Perfect, he comes over to our table sometimes on his breaks from dancing at the other part of the bar that isn't full of noisy theater kids," Terry explained. "Are you down to come with us, or do you have to be at work tomorrow?"

"No, I've got some time. I don't officially start work until next week," I said.

"Good, now drain that Shirley so we can dip," Terry said.

I drank the rest of my cocktail and then the group, led by Terry, headed over to this Sanctuary place. This was the beginning of what I would later describe to my friends back home as emotional whiplash. Not even a full month prior, I was back to being unemployed and living with my parents, not knowing what to do next with my life. Now, I was not only living in Los Angeles but also somehow got instantly connected to a group of gays, good gays, that reminded me of my theater friends back home. Still not knowing what to expect, fear of the unknown morphed into excitement of what could be possible.

We got to the bar where I could already hear show tunes blasting from inside. I flashed my driver's license to a very friendly security guard at the entrance.

"Oh, she still gets carded, must be nice," Dylan said to me, sarcastically.

"Be nice and go order this sweet boy another Dirty Shirley," Terry said, giving his credit card to Dylan.

*Is this a trap? Are these guys actually being nice? Or did they just lure me in with show tunes and free drinks? Tomorrow morning, I'm going to wake up half-naked in the park without a kidney, right? Nah, too many witnesses.*

Walking into the bar was like walking into a chocolate factory for the first time. Everything was so colorful, the televisions were high quality, the floors were surprisingly clean, and there were a ton of theater lovers all sitting at tables watching clips of various musicals on the monitors.

"So, this is how our show tunes night works," Terry explained. "The first part of it, we do a sort of Rocky Horror style performance with those performers over there in the corner. See those props behind them? That's a dress-up box with wigs, costumes, and various props. They'll act out whatever scene is up there on the screen and lip sync along."

"That sounds so ridiculous. I love it," I said.

"It is! And then afterward we do showtunes karaoke, but make sure to get your name in early because the line gets super long super quickly. Since you're a first timer, I'll have Dylan get you up higher on the list," Terry explained.

"Here's your Shirley. Such an auspicious drink for someone about to pop his showtunes cherry," Dylan said.

"My showtunes cherry has been popped many times before, thank you very much," I joked back.

We headed over to a large table in the back of the room. I would later learn that Terry was one of the original attendees of this little musical night when it first started, so he and his friends sat at a reserved table every week. The group ordered nachos, sliders, and a variety of finger foods for us all to share.

Not long after, we were approached by the promoter for the event, Maya, a charming Welsh woman with a vibrant personality and hair that resembled Bernadette Peters. She could not have been more friendly and welcoming.

"A newbie! We love newbies! Welcome, welcome, handsome. We're so happy you're here. Tell me your favorite song, and we will put you at the very top of the karaoke list. I'll have to bump some divas off the list, but you're worth it, gorgeous," Maya said.

*Ok, what the actual fuck is going on here? Food and drinks? Welcoming people? Musical theater? There is no way this is happening. I've been miserable all day, every day for half a year, and then I move to the supposed vapid capital of the world? This is L.A. I thought everyone in here would have identical faces and*

*waist sizes, but they don't; just a group of fun theater people living in the moment.*
*No one is trying to impress each other, they're just trying to have fun. This feels*
*like...home? Is this like reverse karma or a dream or something because holy shit.*

Terry's table was large, and people shuffling in and out seemed to know at least one person in this group.

"I feel like a mafia wife," I joked to Terry.

"Well, you know how the song goes: when you're good to mama..." Terry started singing.

"Mama's good to you!" we both sang and began giggling.

Here's the thing with theater people: it doesn't matter if you're 5, 15, or 50 years old, you are going to quote lyrics from musicals and apply them to your everyday life until the day you die.

"Hey there, sexy, we have a newbie in the house tonight," Terry said to a scantily clad guy who walked up to our table, looking very sexy indeed.

I turned around, and my eyes locked on a handsome Latin man who I assumed was the Carlos that they were all friends with. He was dripping with sweat from dancing on the other side of the bar, but, as promised, had come over on his break. He had dollar bills popping out of his glittery briefs with the bar's name branded on the waistband. He had very smooth, unblemished copper-brown skin and a very sexy, toned body. His most muscular features were his calves, which fit tightly into a pair of tall, glittery high heels. A go-go wearing high heels, how about that?

"Hey baby, nice to meet you," Carlos said, kissing me on both cheeks. "Sorry, I'm super sweaty, it's a busy crowd for a weekday."

"This one speaks Spanish, too," Terry said, hyping me up.

"Aye! Bebé, que bueno!" Carlos said.

"Well, I'm kind of losing my Spanish, but maybe I could get some help getting it back," I said with a little wink.

"Aye, Papa, don't start something you can't finish," Carlos said, blushing and fanning himself.

"He's also a dancer," Terry added.

"A dancer? You came to L.A. to dance, Papi?" he asked.

"Well, I kind of came to L.A. to restart my life, dancing is just how I'm planning to pay the bills for now," I said.

"No, Papa, you need to sell it! Don't doubt yourself. You're sexy, and if you want to dance here, you've got to own it, baby," Carlos said.

"Yeah, listen to the queen," Terry chimed in.

I began explaining to Carlos and Terry that, while I did not have any honed dancing skills, I was more than willing to learn and do whatever it took to get booked. Carlos learned about my job situation and my very brief history with dancing.

"Ok, Papa. I'm going to give you my number so you can text me, and I'll introduce you to Charlie, who does a lot of the bookings at bars here. Just send him some sexy photos of you, but no nudes, though. He doesn't book for here, we have our auditions every month. You just missed the November one, so you'll have to come next month," Carlos explained. "If you need, I can help you do some sexy dancing, guapo."

"Well, that sounds fantastic, I appreciate it," I said.

*Oh, great. Another slutty Footloose montage is pending.*

"When's your break over?" Terry asked.

"Um, three minutes ago," Carlos giggled. "Tengo que irme, it was so nice to meet you, papi. I'm off at ten, and I'll send your info to Charlie. Besitos, Papa."

With that, Carlos strutted off fabulously in his high heels, with his sexy, toned booty bopping from side to side. I will neither confirm nor deny that he came over and spent the night at my apartment a few nights later.

The rest of the evening went as well as the first part of the evening. The cabaret part of the show was so goofy and silly; I laughed harder and sang louder than I had in months. I sang my karaoke song after a very warm, positive introduction from the emcee of the karaoke portion of the night, who had been tipped off by Maya and Terry that there was a newbie in the house. By the time I left, it was long past midnight, but Santa Monica Boulevard was still packed with people. After escorting me to my car, Terry gave me a big hug and his phone number.

"If you ever need anything, that's the number to call, handsome," he said. "Drive carefully and text me when you're home safe."

We shared a final hug and parted ways.

I drove home feeling elated, my happiness level was definitely over 30. I looked at myself in the rearview mirror and thought that maybe it was time to raise that threshold a little higher, to maybe 50 or 60.

*Am I starting to feel better? Is this what I was missing out on?*

# CHAPTER 9

## WHICH WAY TO THE STAGE?

Los Angeles is not known for rainy weather. The name "City of Angels" evokes a heavenly picture of bright blue skies and light fluffy clouds cascading across the sunlight. The day of my audition was not one of those days. This cold and rainy mid-December morning was one in which I could hear the rain pounding down heavily from inside my room before I even opened my eyes.

I woke up around nine o'clock in the morning to allow myself plenty of time to get to the club for the audition. My theater director from back home loved to say that if you're early, you're on time, and if you're on time, you're late. As best I can, I have tried to live out this motto, especially in instances like these where the stakes were so high. Since the Sanctuary, as I had been taught, was one of the biggest, if not the biggest, gay bars in West Hollywood, I put a lot of pressure on myself to nail this audition. Sure, there could have been other work opportunities, but given my lack of luck in finding a job at the bars on my first visit, I did not want to take any chances.

It was very dark inside my room. Any other day, I would have relaxed and stared at the ceiling; today was different. I wasted no time getting out of bed. Two of my loud barking roommates charged at me and then sniffed my feet on my walk from my bedroom to the kitchen to make myself a fruit smoothie. I caught a glimpse of the gray, gloomy morning that awaited me outside through the sliding glass door that led out to our balcony. I crawled onto the couch as I sipped my smoothie, staring outside at the gloomy gray sky. The sun was desperately trying to deliver light past a cluster of ominous dark clouds.

*Me too, sun. Me too.*

The past few weeks had been a whirlwind. My teaching job was off to a great start, I had reduced my drinking frequency significantly, and I was slowly but surely growing my little friend group at the weekly musical theater night. I also joined a few other organizations, including a Taiwanese networking group, and began volunteering to teach civics in Spanish to people preparing to take their citizenship exams. My routine had become stable, and I was settling in comfortably in my new home; now all that was left was securing the side hustle.

After I finished my smoothie, I returned to my bedroom and prepared my dancing attire for the audition. Repeatedly, I had to keep reminding myself that this audition was for my finances and not my ego. I felt excited that this audition even carried the potential to be on stage again, but this was L.A. and not the Central Valley; I knew that the competition would be far more intense. There would certainly be boys there who would be fiercely competitive, in the best possible physical shape, and ready with their A-game. Indeed, I wasn't that dorky 12-year-old kid with zero dance abilities, but I also was not professionally trained as a dancer, as I assumed many people auditioning would be.

Fortunately, Carlos had come over to my house a few times at the beginning of the month to give me pointers just as Javier had. The pointers he gave me were not too different: you're sexy, but we can tell which continent your ancestors are from based on how you dance. Since Carlos had danced at Sanctuary for many years, he knew the kind of dancing that would earn me a spot and what I should wear. The pointers were helpful, so I didn't feel like I was rushing into something without any preparation. His assistance, combined with Rita's breathing exercises, helped temper my anxieties. Showtime.

As soon as I pulled out of the parking garage, I blasted my windshield wipers to the highest possible setting that I could, and yet could still not see very well outside. Water was pouring through the gutters like Niagara Falls, and I immediately went into survival mode. Angelenos are infamous for forgetting how to drive when it rains, and the last thing I needed now was both a car accident to pay for and a potential financial opportunity lost. Fortunately, people avoid the roads like the plague on days like this, which render them empty. My intrusive thoughts, however, were harder to avoid.

*This is it for you, buddy. You make too much money to qualify for welfare but not enough to feed yourself. If you screw up this audition, you might have to sell your ass on Vaseline alley. You're going to have to learn how to bottom if you want to survive in this town.*

Time to blast the radio. Be gone, intrusive thoughts!

I finally made it to the Sanctuary. Typically, when I go to the bars in WeHo, I park in a covered public parking lot located around the corner. I love strolling through the park on my way to the bars to enjoy a few final moments of tranquility before I enter the raucous, loud bars. The walk back to my car also serves as a peaceful cooldown afterward.

Today was a different day, though. I had no interest in getting myself, particularly my shoes, soaking wet before a dance audition. There are a few parking spaces on the curbs right outside the bars that provide 2-hour parking, but, of course, they are almost always occupied.

*Not today, Satan!*

Continuing to coast on my good luck streak, there was a perfect parking spot directly outside the Sanctuary. Jackpot! My excitement quickly faded to annoyance when the stupid parking meter took its sweet-ass time processing my debit card. To make matters worse, I could barely see the stupid little screen indicating whether or not my payment went through. I just stood there trying to shield my shoes as best I could with my crappy little umbrella.

*You should have brought an extra pair of shoes, dummy. Or brought your boots. Use your head, I thought you had a master's degree? Ok, shut up, that's enough out of you. I need to prepare for this audition but goddammit why won't this stupid parking meter—oh wait, there it goes. Yay.*

I ran into the Sanctuary completely drenched from head to toe, and must have looked like a mess because the entire wait staff looked at me like I was a stray puppy that had lost its way. They also seemed confused as to why I was there, and as I looked around, I realized that their expressions of confusion weren't meritless. Looking at the vast space, I noticed that there was not a single person in the bar who was not an employee.

*Am I the only one auditioning today? That would be sweet! No competition. Wait a minute, that means more attention is going to be on me, which could be a bad thing. Ok, back to breathing.*

I meandered around the bar in my squeaking sneakers to try and find anyone who knew where the audition was. After circling the bar a few times, I encountered a well-dressed silver fox who seemed perplexed to see me.

"Hi, my name is DJ," I said, extending my hand to the gentleman.

"Hi there, DJ. I'm Tim," he said, still looking at me slightly skeptically for being there before noon on such a stormy day.

"Um, I was just curious, where exactly do I need to report for the dancing audition?" I inquired, eying over his shoulder to view a nearly empty club.

"Audition? Oh, you mean the go-go audition they're hosting later tonight?" Tim asked.

*Way to go, Einstein. It's 11 PM, not 11 AM who the hell would have an audition for a nightlife job at 11 in the morning? Well, I don't know, maybe to screen people before they go on stage? You probably look really stupid right now, so you need to play it off so this guy doesn't think you're a complete moron.*

"Oh, yeah! I was wondering, when I show up later tonight, where I should go?" I said.

*Nice save.*

"Certainly, you're going to want to arrive a little bit after ten o'clock, and the person you're going to want to look for is named

Jaden. Just ask one of the bartenders to point him out to you when you arrive, and they'll help you out from there," he said.

"Thank you so much, I'm new here, so I'm still trying to get my bearings," I said.

"Oh, very nice. Where did you move from?" he said warmly.

*Let's see, I've lived everywhere and have bounced around to more places in this country than I care to name in the course of a polite conversation, but ok.*

"I'm from the Central Valley of California, kind of right in the middle of it," I responded. "I have been sort of nomadic for the past few years, but I decided I wanted to stay put in one city for longer than just a couple of years, so here I am."

"Well, you picked a great city to move to. I'm from the Midwest originally, but I've been here for quite a while, so I'm practically an Angeleno," he said.

"That's great! I love it so far, even though this is not the weather I was promised in the brochure," I joked while gesturing outside.

"Well, you have fun tonight, I wish you the best of luck. I've got to get back to the kitchen to do some work," he said.

"Thank you very much. I appreciate it!" I said, shaking his hand, and then immediately left.

*Sheesh, that was like diffusing a live hand grenade. That could have gone much worse than that, way to stick the landing. Now you've got the intel, now you can come back prepared and kick some ass. No matter, just another 12 hours of these nerves and I'm going to be good to go on stage.*


I showed up to the audition early again, just before 10. It did not seem like any different night at the Sanctuary: people were filing in and finding their friends, singles were looking sexier than normal, hoping to attract someone special, and both bartenders and barbacks were enjoying the calm before the storm.

The nerves I felt toward the audition had been simmering deep in my gut all day. If I haven't made this clear enough, before I began go-go dancing, I had never been nervous before an audition. The stage had always been my happy place, but this was different. I wasn't just vying for a role as I had back in my theater days; this was vying for grocery money.

The pressure began to build, and I started to feel sick; I felt like I was going to throw up. After a while, I ran to the bathroom and *did* throw up. Not eating much during the day helped reduce the amount of time spent heaving into the toilet, but I still felt gross and helpless. I began to slow my breathing again, Rita's help coming in clutch again. After taking some very slow, deep breaths, I closed my eyes and thought about Damien. I pictured him beaming at me with his signature look. My nerves began to slowly subside, and I felt much more peaceful and grounded. Even beyond the grave, Damien was warming my heart and soul while boosting my confidence.

I flushed, washed my hands, and rinsed my mouth out with the mouthwash provided in the men's room.

I found myself a stool to sit on at the bar, allowing myself the chance to reflect on how I would not be here if it weren't for Jordy, Gavin, and Damien, but especially Damien, being so adamant that I pursue this. All I could think about was performing that night and watching him give me the look. *That* was the person I was going to perform for tonight.

Finally, the clock struck 10:30. Walking in a somewhat rushed fashion was Jaden, a tall, handsome, clean-cut gentleman who, as I quickly learned, was the manager of the dancers.

"Hi, I'm DJ, I'm here to audition," I said confidently.

"Hello there, handsome! I'm Jaden. Welcome to the Sanctuary, have you visited us before?" Jaden said after giving me a warm hug.

"A few times, yeah. I've been to the show tunes night a lot," I said.

"Perfect, that's awesome. Well, we're all going to get started by having a little meeting with the candidates before we get started, so if you could just hang out around here, we're going to get started in about 15," Jaden said. "Is there anything else you need from me before I step outside for a moment?"

"No, I should be good, thanks!" I said.

Jaden disappeared around the corner. With fifteen minutes to spare, I began to analyze my competition. The group of auditionees was diverse in terms of skill level and physical appearance. At least two of the guys looked like they spent all day, every day at the gym and could even compete as bodybuilders. There was a group of three handsome guys who were speaking to each other in some Slavic language that I could not discern. It's still not clear, but at the time, I wasn't sure if their isolating themselves from the rest of the group was because they didn't speak very much English or because they were straight. Then there were a few others who varied in appearance and garb.

Jaden called all the candidates together near the front of the tiny dressing room to give us a rundown of the evening.

"Ok, girlies, if I could have your undivided attention for just a few minutes, thank you. So the way this goes is that Carlos over here is going to call each of your names, and then you'll have two minutes up on the platforms," Jaden explained.

*Wait, Carlos? My Carlos? Seriously? He's running the show? Holy crap, this is too good to be true, why didn't he tell me that he's also a judge? I guess he didn't want to influence me, but who cares? This is brilliant!*

"Once you're done, Carlos is going to make sure you each get a final round of applause. After each of you is done auditioning, the judges are going to narrow down their top three choices, and then you will have a sudden death round like on RuPaul. Then, the audience will applaud for their favorite, and based on who gets the loudest response, the winner will be our new resident dancer," Jaden said.

*Yikes. There must be at least a dozen dudes here. These guys are all hot and look super competitive. Are they intimidated, too? Am I the only one who feels like this? Fuck, am I going to throw up again? Whatever, focus!*

"Now, if you do not win tonight, please do not panic! We have booked dancers here before who have not won. All we ask is that you are sober and respectful, and please do not show pole or hole. Be as freaky as you want, just be clean. Make sense, boys?" Jaden asked while raising his thumbs for additional confirmation.

We all nodded our heads in agreement, and Jaden vanished a second time.

"Hello, my babies, I'm Carlos. I will post the order of when you go on right now in the dressing room. Please and thank you, do not all go in at once, this dressing room is muy poquito and I might love a bunch of men inside *me* all at once, but she doesn't," Carlos said, referring to the dressing room itself. "So please go in no more than 2 at a time, there are already some of our other dancers inside, so please be like a toxic top, go in and go out, ok guapos?"

All of us, except for the European boys, chuckled. I winked at Carlos as he made his way out. The contestants started going into the room two at a time. By the time it was my turn, I nervously scanned the list of eleven candidates. I was contestant number 6. From my days in theater and competitive speech and debate, I've been overly paranoid about how the order can affect the outcome, at least marginally. Trying to stop thinking about it, I ventured out of the dressing room and began stretching. I convinced myself that it didn't matter whether I was at the beginning of the lineup or the end, I was going to put in 150%. I headed to the dance floor to do a little bit of reconnaissance.

The setup was pretty standard for a gay bar. There was a large dance floor in the middle surrounded by two elevated L-shaped platforms mirroring each other. The corners of the L on either side of the dance floor had a pole that was optional to perform tricks or sexy moves on.

As I kept doing my methodical research on how I was going to make sure I worked every square foot of that stage, I felt a hard slap on my left butt cheek followed immediately by a hug from behind.

"Oh my god, what are you all doing here?" I said to Terry, who had arrived at the bar with Dylan and a few other friends from the showtunes crowd.

"Duh, we're here to support our new sexy friend. We're a little late because we had to go to the ATM to get your dollar bills. You didn't think I was just going to not bring a big group to cheer for you, did you?" Terry said with a wink.

Touched, I gave him another big hug.

"Oh, and by the way, we're going to sit at the table that's closest to the stage, so if you can at some point, try to drop your balls on Dylan's face," Terry joked.

"I will certainly do that, you pervert!" I laughed.

"Awesome, I already ordered you a couple of shots for good luck," Terry said.

"You are so sweet," I said.

"Yeah, it's going to make you dance super sexy, and we are so here for it," Dylan said loudly to my face.

"Wow, buddy you smell very flammable, don't let this bitch anywhere near the fireplace, you guys," I joked. "I appreciate the drinks, but I can't stay out too late, I've got to catch a flight to Denver tomorrow morning."

"Off to see the fam?" Terry asked.

"Yeah, and a few friends. But I'll be back for New Year's Eve," I said.

"Great. Well, I ordered the rest of us vodka sodas and water for this one," Terry said, glaring passive-aggressively at Dylan. "Anyways, are you nervous at all?"

"Well, I kind of am a little bit. I don't normally get nervous before an audition, but the stakes are kind of high now," I said.

"Do you get sick when you're nervous?" Dylan slurred.

"Actually, I did get sick," I confessed.

"Oh no, sweet boy. Are you ok?" Terry asked.

"Yeah, I'm fine," I said. "I was nervous all day, so I didn't eat very much."

"Wait, is that how you're able to look like—" Dylan said as he gestured at my body.

"Yeah, blink twice if it is because that's not a good way to go, sweet boy," Terry said, looking concerned.

"No, I'm fine. It's just nerves, a lot is on the line, and I think it's just getting to my head," I said.

Terry kept his eyes on me to make sure that I was telling the truth, which I was. Body dysmorphia is a big problem in the gay community, and a lot of boys go to extreme lengths to try and look thin and toned. I've had the opposite problem and have always wanted not to look skinny, but I wasn't going to go to the other extreme to fix *that* problem either. Rita had just helped me fix my rage, no reason I should make it go back up just to look jacked. No roids for me.

"How many bars have you danced at?" Dylan asked.

I started explaining my go-go journey from dancing, starting with Jordy.

"Wait, so the guy who knew you couldn't dance was the one who booked you?" Dylan asked bluntly, eliciting another glare from Terry. "I mean, you know what I mean. How did that happen?"

I told them the rest of my story. I didn't leave anything out: my sexy trip to Europe, my spiral into depression, the phone call from the suicide hotline, my month in Palm Springs and the safari nightmare, running around Manhattan and the intern, losing Damien while I was in Mexico, my brief stint in Mississippi, wobbling emotionally in Denver, coming back to California to rebuild my life, and then finally moving down to LA.

Gauging from the reaction of Terry's friends, I realized that I had perhaps shared too much. None of them gave me the "time out" gesture like Rita did.

*Nice going, blabbermouth. You made new friends and now they're going to leave your ass.*

Just the opposite. Terry looked me in the eyes and held my hand.

"We've got your back, sweet boy. We're so happy you crashed our table," he said.

Trying not to get too emotional, I thanked him and the rest of the crew for being there to support me. This same kind of community support was what I had all along back home, and now I had it here.

*Toxic bitches are everywhere, but so are cool bitches.*

Eventually, the group made their way through the club and got a table, as they said, very close to the platform. It was beginning to feel real. Nervous though I still was over having to essentially dance for sustenance, having people in my corner attending in the audience was a major boost I needed.

It was time to compete.

"Good evening bitches, welcome to the Sanctuary, how are we all doing tonight?" Carlos bellowed into the microphone to a vibrant applause from the audience. "You are here on a very special night because tonight you will help us decide which sexy go-go will take the top prize and be our new resident dancer!"

The audience continued whooping and hollering.

*Please, god, tell me some of those screams are Terry and his friends.*

"First contestant of the night, can we have Dr. Screws-a-lot?" Carlos shouted.

Yes, you read that correctly. Go-go dancers have stage names, and some sound like that. I'm as shocked as you are.

Well, let me tell you, Dr. Screws-a-lot lived up to his title. I'm not sure he had a medical license, but he was an absolute hunk with a perfectly chiseled body, a decent bulge, and a handsome face. He was not a particularly gifted dancer, but I was in no position to judge, and tonight was certainly not the night to test karma.

After a few performers competed, my brain went into academic mode and categorized each of the performers into three circles that occasionally would overlap as they would in a Venn diagram. Frustratingly, I could not just turn my brain off and be a regular person and watch the damn competition; I had to perform a bloody academic analysis of the dancers.

The first category of dancers was those blessed with good looks; this included guys who looked just naturally beautiful and those who looked like they worked very hard on their bodies. This group honestly did not have to do very much in terms of movement because they were so fun to look at. They could get a large amount of tips just by swaying back and forth like a mechanical character on a theme park ride.

The second category included those who were gifted at dancing, either by formal classes or professional experience. These were the dancers who were able to do pole tricks, twerk, and even breakdance.

It is typical for these types of dancers to wear knee pads to perform a variety of dance moves.

The final category was the "fun people." They, and when I say they I mean we, are not particularly gifted at dancing nor able to perform any particularly interesting tricks with the pole or otherwise. But goddammit, that group is by far the most fun!

*Sexy is temporary, fun is timeless!*

Each of these three groups overlapped occasionally; some people could dance well and be attractive, but not necessarily be fun; some people were attractive and fun, etc. Doubt came seeping back in.

*So, if I were to win the competition or at least leave a solid first impression, would I need to be a triple threat and be at the center of the Venn diagram?*

I quickly slapped that idea down in my head to not distract me from my two-minute audition, which was quickly approaching. Dancer number two went by, followed by dancer three, and then dancer four.

As dancer number five was completing his performance, I can't even remember why, but I just remember feeling incredibly calm. Of all times to turn off the nerves, I'm glad it was then.

"Ok, thank you, Big Tony. Give it up for Big Tony, everyone!" Carlos cheered.

Yeah. He lived up to *his* name as well.

"Up next, can we get DJ to the stage, please? Where's DJ? DJ going once?" Carlos called out, looking around.

"Here! I'm right here," I said, rushing up to the edge of the platform and waving over at Carlos, who was in the DJ booth.

"Aye, Dios Mio, a go-go named DJ? How fabulous! Alright, everyone, let's give up for DJ!" Carlos hooted like a very effeminate wrestling announcer.

With my signature happy-go-lucky style, I threw my arms in the air and started shaking my hips. I waved and winked at various members of the audience as I strutted across the L-shaped stage slowly. The music was so loud, the lights were so bright, and smoke surrounded me on every side. A remix of Rihanna's "Rude Boy" was the song that played primarily through my 2-minute set. It isn't the easiest song to dance to, but the other DJ in the room made sure to remix it in a manner that was more conducive for dancing. It could have been way worse, it could have been "Ease on Down the Road."

I strutted seductively toward my group of friends, who were hooting and hollering with multiple dollar bills stretched out. Squatting down for them to drop some dollar bills into my underwear, I realized Dylan was not even there for me to place my balls on! I learned later that his dumbass went to the bathroom during the middle part of my performance. What a missed opportunity. Nevertheless, I showed the best possible moves I could, trying to show that I had a style and somewhat of a range, but not being too daring with any tricks or anything. That was until I spotted the pole at the end of the platform.

*Fuck it. No guts, no glory.*

I reached up and grabbed the pole, lifted both my legs off the ground, and held on like a koala. Now, what people had failed to warn me before this was that some dancing poles are immobile, and some can spin. This one freaking spun.

*Wait, stop. Stop! How do I stop? Fuck! It's getting faster. Don't fall! Oh my god, I'm going to shoot out into the crowd. Jesus, save me. I feel like I'm going to throw up again. Just land, land!*

By the grace of whoever was watching down on me, I planted my feet on the ground and was able to play it off in a seductive way. I really wish I had popped a Dramamine before I went on.

Working the entire platform, I had so much adrenaline and energy carrying me throughout the rest of my set. I did the few moves I could, complete with plenty of winking and smiles, playing to the audience. When my time was up, I felt like I was only up there for a total of five seconds. It went by so quickly, and then I was off.

"So sexy! Let's hear it for DJ the go-go!" Carlos shouted.

I had very little time to process my two-minute set. The blinding lights from the stage had obscured my vision and nearly caused me to fall over as I made my way down the steps into the crowd. My breathing was heavy, and I was completely drenched in sweat from head to toe; you would be surprised at how much sweat one can accumulate in just two minutes.

My friends were applauding me as I approached their table. High fives, kisses, and sweaty hugs greeted me on my return to the table. A full glass of water with lemon was passed over to me, and I immediately downed it in less than ten seconds.

"Yes, bitch! Work!" Dylan screamed at the top of his lungs, still slightly tipsy.

"Fabulous job, sexy boy!" Terry screamed into my ear.

I sat down, trying to catch my breath. Another ice-cold water with lemon came my way, and I, again, gulped it down quickly. We watched the remaining five contestants perform, and then there was a ten-minute break for the judges to deliberate. But I was impatient, I wanted immediate feedback.

"Ok, hand to God, I want to know: how was I?" I asked the group. "Don't spare my feelings, please, I honestly want to know how I did.

The faces sitting around the table before me all indicated to me that they were still in supportive mode, uninterested in offending their new friend.

"Go for it, hit me with your best shot," I said. "Seriously, after the year I've had, I can take the heat."

"Well, we were very impressed by your audition," Terry said.

*Oh god. I must have done terribly. He's just too nice to offend me. This was a bad idea. I should have spent more time with Carlos before I decided to show myself in this club. Ugh!*

"But?" I asked, trying to ascertain the truth, the whole truth, and nothing but the truth out of his mouth.

"Well, I mean, there *were* some guys with, shall we say, more conventionally fit bodies," Terry said.

He was looking at me like a parent looks at their kid when they have to tell them their goldfish died. Fortunately, this was an observation with which I already concurred and had no problem admitting even before the competition.

"And, well, I think it was pretty clear that you're not a trained dancer," he continued.

Again, no disagreements from me.

"But," he emphasized, "you were by far, *by far,* the most energetic and engaging. On that score, nobody was even a close second."

In my peripheral vision, I could see his friends nodding in agreement.

"A lot of the other contestants were talented and sexy, but they were playing *at* the audience, and you were playing *to* the audience. Does that make sense?" he asked.

*Ok, I'm definitely in category three, then. At least I fit in somewhere.*

This made me feel better, overall; I asked for a blunt analysis, and I got one.

"It makes perfect sense. And honestly, I agree. I know I'm not a triple threat," I said.

Terry looked at me, very confused.

"What do you mean? You *are* a triple threat," he said emphatically.

I looked back at him, mirroring the same confused look he had given me.

"You've got the sexy abs, a sexy bulge, and a handsome face," he said. "I'd say that's a triple threat."

Blushing slightly, I rolled my eyes playfully and started sipping the third glass of water that came around.

It was time for the judges to make their decision. Sudden death was imminent.

The adrenaline from my two-minute set remained strong by the time Carlos came on stage to announce the final three candidates; my nerves were numbed initially, but as soon as he looked down at the card with the final three candidates on it, the butterflies came charging back with a vengeance.

Carlos announced the first contestant, not me. He announced the second contestant, also not me. I began to feel my heartbeat pulsating in a manner that made me feel it up to my ears. Final contestant, not me. My heart sank. I would not be moving on to the final round.

Fortunately for my mood, I remembered what Jaden had said about booking multiple dancers, and yet I immediately felt the hands of my friends around the table patting me on my shoulders and back.

The clock was approaching 1 AM, and my flight was set to leave the next morning at 7:30 AM for Denver. The window of time to get at least *some* sleep was narrowing, I had to make a break for it. After the sudden death competition was over and the winner was chosen, I went back to the dressing room to get my stuff. Miraculously, Carlos stopped me before I could leave.

"Hey, Papi, you did so great tonight!" he said, hugging me and kissing me on both cheeks.

"Yeah, I tried my best," I said with a smile and a shrug.

"No, you were like so much fun to watch. The audience was loving it," he said.

"Thanks, cutie," I said.

*Apparently, the judges didn't agree. Ok, stop being a bitch, things could still turn around.*

Carlos got very close to me and whispered into my ear.

"Ok, what you want to do now is go over to Jaden and thank him for the audition. Be polite and charming like you usually are, and then see what happens," Carlos said.

I nodded and gave Carlos one big final hug, collected my belongings, and walked back into the club to find Jaden. Once I found him, I gave him a big hug and thanked him for the evening.

"Thank you so much for tonight, I appreciate it. Do you think I should—"

Jaden, to my relief, interrupted me.

"Get my number? Absolutely!" he exclaimed.

*Wait, what? You want my number? For real? Holy shit. This is absolutely not what I was expecting. I didn't even make the top three, like, oh my god.*

I thought that I had died and gone to heaven and back. After a year of feeling like I had to beg and plead for a job or even a bloody interview, someone was asking *me* for *my* personal information. And to dance? At one of the most popular bars in WeHo? I was shaking as I struggled to conceal my euphoria. We exchanged numbers, and I gave him a big hug again.

"Perfect. I've got your number! We'll be in touch," Jaden said.

*No. No. No!. I want my good feelings back, goddammit.*

"We'll be in touch" are the worst four words in the English

language, particularly in Los Angeles. What it means is that you are the very last person on the waiting list and that when people are done with whatever other options, they will come scraping for you at the bottom of the barrel.

*Ok, shut up, you're overreacting. He probably will book you, he just needs to get some second opinions. Oh, yeah, second opinions like the jackasses in Denver that said I was sexy but danced too comically? Who cares? He has your number, and he knows Carlos, that's a start.*

Nevertheless, I began to doubt myself again. Jaden was an incredibly affable, professional guy, and I was impressed by the way he managed the audition. Still, with the year I had, I lowered my expectations and made sure not to get my hopes up. Some might call this being a Debbie Downer, I call it growth.

Back in my car, I paused for a moment. The feelings I had been wrestling with before the audition began to subside. Even the doubts I had after the audition did not dampen my spirits, and I couldn't figure out why. My financial situation had not changed, I had not been officially booked, and I had no indication when I would be.

I paid my parking fee at the exit, turned onto Santa Monica, and began to reminisce on the evening. I think that I felt better because I knew, regardless of whether I got booked, I had found a good group of supportive people. Terry and his crew showed up at 11:00 PM on a weeknight for a boy they barely knew, listened attentively to his story, and showered him with support and dollar bills.

That boy was me. I felt incredibly lucky, I began to smile and wept a small tear of gratitude.

By the time I crossed Fairfax Avenue, my smile had vanished. The bumpiness of the road reminded me of the bumpy roads in Mexico when I was blissfully unaware that Damien was having his chest cut open in a room full of doctors attempting to save his life. Tears of gratitude turned to those of sorrow, and then to tears of resentment and anger. Any single one of those friends who came to support me that night could be dead tomorrow, for whatever reason. I could lose any one of my new friends to a heart attack, a hate crime, a shooting, an overdose, suicide, a car crash, or any other kind of tragedy. The feeling that I could lose a friend at any moment had not been erased, but as I got closer to home, I thought about how the support and love I felt from Damien had not left me, even though he was no longer with us. He was there that night with me, in spirit. Memories of that night at Flash had propelled my energy during that audition and calmed my nerves. After a few more slow, deep breaths, my tears returned to those of gratitude as I returned to my apartment and went to sleep.

# CHAPTER 10

# HAPPY NEW YEAR

There is nothing I hate more than hearing my alarm go off after only three hours of sleep. The loud rainfall outside accompanied the loud noises from my intensely vibrating phone. I growled grumpily as I tried to fashion myself a little cocoon with my covers. I felt like I was having the most sober hangover of my life after a loud, exhausting night at the club. After pounding the snooze button for the fifth and final time, it was time for me to wake up and head to the airport.

The whiplash over the past few months had been exciting but overwhelming; I was fully ready to head to the airport to spend a nice Christmas with my family and take a break from L.A. for a few days. To this day, I love L.A., but I also love taking occasional breaks from L.A.

Since I am a California boy through and through, I had a hard time packing for sub-zero weather. I rummaged through my underwear drawer; there were plenty of jocks, thongs, briefs, trunks, but no Long-Johns to be found. I packed lightly since I'd only be gone for about a week, and most of the time I'd be sporting sweatpants inside. I threw on a pair of jeans and the sweatshirt from my alma mater and got ready. As I finished the last of my packing, I stumbled upon the outfit Enrique had gifted me when I was in Denver the previous summer. I smiled to myself, held the outfit close to my chest, then tossed it back into the drawer with my other go-go garments.

After my plane descended rather turbulently into Denver, I was greeted by two very eager cousins, Kiana and Kristen, at baggage claim. As per usual, they hugged me as hard as they possibly could, almost like I was a pimple they intended to pop. We exited the airport only to be greeted by Colorado's notorious biting winter freeze. As much as I would have loved living in Denver, I like dressing like a surfer in December and not an Eskimo.

We turned the corner out of the busy parking lot and made our way north on I-25, taking advantage of the time we had alone to chat.

"So, what's this side job you keep hinting at?" Kiana asked impatiently.

"Well, I've been keeping a low profile about it because I don't know how far it's going to go, but yesterday I auditioned to be a go-go dancer at a club in West Hollywood," I said.

"Wait, a what?" Kristen asked with a slight chuckle.

"A go-go dancer," I repeated.

"Isn't that like...a stripper?" Kiana asked, trying to conceal a giggle.

*Here we go again, this is like Friendsgiving, round two.*

"Not quite," I said before giving my married, heterosexual cousins the same lecture I had given my married, heterosexual friends.

"Well, you'll have to show us your dance moves when we get home," Kiana said.

"Yeah, *that'll* spread some Christmas cheer," I quipped sarcastically. "I actually auditioned to be a go-go in Denver when I was here for your wedding last summer."

"What?! And you didn't tell us about it!?" Kiana exclaimed, squeezing my shoulders from the back seat.

"Yeah, *that* would have gone over well," I said.

"We would have totally come down to support you! Oh my god, I could have had my bachelorette party there!" Kiana exclaimed.

"Yeah, what a missed opportunity," Kristen said, shaking her head.

"Ok, first of all, do you want to see your cousin 97% naked at your bachelorette party? And secondly, how would that have gone down when the word of mouth spread through the grapevine and made it to the rest of the family?" I said.

"Yeah, you're probably right," Kristen said.

"Besides, if anything, Adam should have come for *his* bachelor party," I teased, referring to Kiana's new husband.

"Back off! He's mine!" Kiana said, slapping my shoulders again.

"Kristen, hold my hoops. Let me at her, let me at her!" I said, pretending to remove my earrings and pick a fight with Kiana. We all laughed before sharing a brief moment of silence.

Kristen kept her left hand on the steering wheel and put her right hand on my knee and squeezed it hard. Kiana put her hands on my shoulders from the back seat.

"We're really happy you're doing ok now. It was a really scary year," Kristen said.

*Yes, and you two don't even know about the suicide hotline or Palm Springs or Mississippi yet.*

"Thanks for providing my mom intel on the back channel, you conniving little sleuths," I joked.

Kristen and Kiana smiled at each other proudly via Kristen's rearview mirror.

"Thanks. We're totally FBI material," Kristen said.

"Pew pew," I said, shooting them both with an imaginary finger gun.

We arrived at my aunt and uncle's house for dinner as the sky began its final transition from dark purple to nearly pitch black.

"Ok, time to go back to pretending that I'm a conservative bachelor who just hasn't met the right girl yet," I joked.

"Ok, but when we go out tomorrow with just the cousins, we want you to go back to being fabulous and show us some of your moves!" Kristen said.

"Yes, just don't do them anywhere near *my* husband!" Kiana warned.

"I don't care who I dance in front of, as long as I get tips," I clapped back.

"*I'll* give you as many tips as you want as long as you don't twerk anywhere near our husbands!" Kiana warned.

"See? I *am* a pretty good businessman," I bragged.

We all laughed as we made our way into the warm, festively decorated house where we were all greeted by excited screams and open arms. We went through the welcome line, hugging every aunt, uncle, cousin, grandparent, in-law, and guest.

I don't see eye to eye with a lot of my family, and there are some around whom I don't feel I can be fully authentic. However, the moment when I arrive back at one of my aunts and uncles' homes to a greeting line, I feel more warm, welcomed, and complete than I ever have on a dance floor at a gay club.

*There's another paradox for you to help me unbox, Rita.*

The next few days were filled with family holiday traditions and activities: sipping cider by the fireplace, cuddling under blankets watching Christmas movies, taking long walks out in the snow, reminiscing about previous holiday shenanigans, and eating—so much eating.

On Christmas night, my final night with family, the power went out at Grandma's house. All the cousins scavenged around for some candles from the basement cupboards, and we lit up the basement and played board games by the candlelight. It was equal parts spontaneous, pleasant, and joyful. It's a memory I cherish deeply to this day.

*You were right, dipshit. Darkness is inevitable; being alone in the darkness is not.*

The day after Christmas, my dad drove me back down to Denver and dropped me off at Enrique's apartment, where I would remain for the last couple of days before I headed back to L.A.

With haste, we headed out to our favorite Thai restaurant for dinner. We ordered the same meals and, as usual, Enrique grabbed the check. After stuffing ourselves with warm yellow curry and eggrolls, we ended up at Chuckie's again for karaoke night. Several months had gone by, and I felt like I had been stuck in a time warp. Thankfully, this time around, I had a steady job and was beginning to build a sustainable social foundation.

The bar was relatively empty when Enrique and I showed up. Multicolored Christmas lights twinkled as they dangled down from the ceiling. The bartenders from the summer were still around, I even recognized a couple of them. Enrique ordered a diet club soda, and I ordered an Appletini.

"Still drinking like a bottom, are we?" Enrique chuckled.

"Why does everyone shit on my drink preferences?" I asked.

"Well, maybe because there isn't much daylight between what you drink and what a 21-year-old sorority girl drinks," he teased.

"Just be glad I'm not drinking straight up vodka without a chaser," I clapped back.

"Touché," he said as he grabbed our drinks and led the way to the table.

We chatted for a bit about his life in Denver and how much he missed the boys back home in California. The grass was truly always greener because I missed my Rocky Mountain cuties.

After a few minutes of chatting, in all her glorious splendor, Celeste Teal emerged from the dressing room like a sparkling diamond. She was wearing a very tight-fitting black sequined dress with very tall, sparkling high heels. Our eyes locked. A little smirk crossed her face, and I couldn't help but blow a kiss over to her. She strutted her way toward me with the confidence that had not waned since I had last seen her.

"Milady," I said, grabbing her hand and kissing the top of her palm.

"Welcome back, gorgeous," she said, air kissing me on both cheeks.

"Well, it must be a day that ends in a 'Y' because you look stunning," I said flirtatiously.

"Oh, stop it! Okay, maybe don't stop, keep going," she said, blushing.

"I can and I think I will," I said, wrapping my arms around her waist.

"You look good!" she said as she started massaging my biceps. "Damn, looks like L.A. has been good to you."

She was right. I was only a few weeks in, but L.A. *had* been good to me. Coming from someone who had seen me when I was at rock bottom, it really meant a lot.

*You can always count on a drag queen to give you a confidence boost.*

"I'm so sorry, but I must excuse myself, Mama needs to get this show on the road," she said, referring to the karaoke night.

"Of course. It's great to see you," I said, winking at her.

"You too, boo," she said back with a wink.

She disappeared briefly backstage while Enrique and I walked up to the DJ booth to put in our song requests. Enrique typically sang something country, and I would sing either a showtune or Sinatra. Due to the low volume of people in the club that night, we were both able to do three of the songs we requested.

We waited a little while longer. After a few minutes, a guest in a hoodie walked into the bar. It was Jake.

"Whoop, twelve o'clock," I said.

Enrique looked directly ahead.

"Not my twelve o'clock, *your* twelve o'clock," I said.

"I'm sorry, I'm a digital bitch not an analog," Enrique joked.

Jake walked over to us. I immediately gave him a hug.

"Hey Jake," I said.

"Hi, DJ," he said.

It looked like he had been crying.

"How have you been? Did you have a nice Christmas?" I asked.

"Yes. I just wanted to let you know, I love you too," he said.

I paused, not knowing how to respond.

"And, I heard what you said. You're the first person to call me out. I have a problem. I need to curb, too, a lot more than you do. I just want to let you know, I'm going to get help," he said.

*This could have totally been you. You were so ridiculously close to being an alcoholic yourself. Don't judge him, don't you fucking dare.*

"I'm glad to hear that. I hope you do, you are a great person. You've been dealt a much more difficult hand than I have. You deserve to hit the jackpot," I said.

"Thank you, DJ," Jake said, holding back tears.

"Take care, keep me posted," I said. "I love you. You're welcome to join us for karaoke."

"I'd love to," he said.

"Ok, honeys, we have a very special guest here tonight in Denver, all the way from Los Angeles, California. Singing for us here at Chuckie's for one night only, my very sexy go-go friend, DJ!" she exclaimed into the microphone.

Enrique made up 80% of the applause volume as I headed for the stage. Celeste Teal kissed me again on both cheeks as I took the microphone from her. I looked out at the crowd; it was only a slightly bigger crowd than when I had my go-go audition.

I sang my Sinatra song first. Several of the members of the crowd were on their phones, a few were talking to each other, and the remaining were sipping on their drinks, somewhat paying attention but somewhere else, mentally. As you may have guessed, the only person looking at me with full attention and that massive smile on his face was Enrique. I winked at him as I continued through the song. I looked to my left, and Celeste Teal was watching me as well, fanning herself with her hand.

The rest of the night is a bit of a blur, but I remember singing my lungs out, dancing with Enrique on the dance floor when the crowd picked up slightly, chatting with a couple of other hot visitors, and getting Celeste Teal caught up on my life in L.A. It was a great way to spend the last night of my visit.

Hangovers hit differently when your life is going well. It was a few days before New Year's Eve, and my hangover felt better than my hangover at this point the previous year. I may not have been at the end of the tunnel, but I knew I was at least headed towards a light and not more darkness.

The aroma of Enrique's coffee machine wafted through the entire apartment again. I propped myself up on his couch and let out a big, loud yawn. I stretched a big, satisfying stretch and began rubbing my temples. Enrique, the morning person, emerged from his bedroom in just his underwear and smiled at me with his signature chipper attitude.

"Morning, pudding," he said.

"Morning, cholo," I grumbled.

"How did you sleep, mi angelito?" he asked. "Did you have any fun dreams about those sexy boys from last night?"

"No, but I did dream that you went into work in your underwear and HR gave you a wedgie for being late," I joked, still half asleep.

"No! Wait, was HR at least hot in your dream?" he asked.

We started laughing as we proceeded to plan out the rest of our day, which would end with him driving me to the airport. We laughed and joked a bit more before spending more time reflecting.

"So, any fun plans for New Year's Eve?" he asked.

"Not really," I shrugged. "I have a few new friends that I'll hit up, but I'm sure they're busy with other things. If I don't get invited to something, I'll just hang out with the dogs at home and wake up on New Year's Day and go on a hike or something," I said.

"That sounds fun. When do you hear back about your Sanctuary audition?" he asked.

"Not sure. The guy who books the dancers just got my number and said that we'd be in touch," I said.

"Well, that sounds like a good thing, right?" he asked.

"I hope so," I said with a yawn.

"You seem suspiciously chill for someone who was panicking about the audition just a few days ago," he said.

I shrugged my shoulders.

"Well, I think my first New Year's resolution is to not panic. It's going to be hard, navigating my way in a new city once the shine wears off. But this past year was hard, and I made it this far without crashing and burning. Well, I crashed, but I didn't burn completely," I said. "And I'll tell you something else. My second New Year's resolution is to be way less judgmental of homeless people, hookers, and serial killers."

"Wait, what? Why, pray tell?" he asked with curiosity.

"Because at multiple points this year, I could have become any three of those things. In Mississippi, I almost *did* become all three of those things at once, and I'm not even kidding," I said sternly. "If it weren't for the people I've seen on this trip and my friends back home, my life could have gone a much different direction. I crashed but I didn't burn, which is why I feel as calm as I do now. Because I know who are the real ones I can rely on when shit hits the fan."

"Am I one of them?" Enrique asked.

"No, but you have a cute butt, so I guess I'll keep you around." I teased.

"Ah! You bitch!" he cackled with his signature infectious laughter.

We sat around on the couch for a little while longer watching movies. Then, my phone buzzed.

"Oh my god," I said, covering my mouth.

"What? What is it?" Enrique asked.

I couldn't respond; I was in such a state of shock. Words failed me, yet again.

"What? DJ? Oh my god, DJ? DJ! What is it?" he shouted.

My eyes began to water, and I looked up through tears at Enrique.

"You got booked for New Year's Eve, didn't you?" he asked.

I nodded my head.

"Where?" he asked intently.

I nodded my head again, with a massive grin.

"Fuck yeah!" he yelled, as we started jumping up and down out of excitement. We fell over on the couch. Enrique gave me a big hug and then started smacking me hard on my ass.

"Didn't I tell you that you were going to go places? Didn't I? Why don't you ever listen to papi?" he cackled, continuing to smack my ass as hard as he could.

"Hey, don't bruise the goods! I have to show those off later!" I said, laughing.

I hopped up and began jumping and doing a victory dance around the kitchen with Enrique before immediately responding to Jaden. I told him I was in. He gave me the call time and details before wishing me a splendid rest of my holidays. Needing to catch my breath, I plopped down with Enrique on the couch.

Fighting back tears, I looked at Enrique, the friend who had held my hand and consoled me when I was a nervous wreck after my Denver audition. Now, he was holding my hand out of congratulations and not consolation.

"Thank you," I said, as a single teardrop trickled down my right cheek.

"No, thank *you*. And you know what? Chuckie's could have had a bad bitch," Enrique joked.

We hugged a deep, long hug. How amazing that hug felt is impossible to put into words.


December 31, 2023, what a night. I didn't know if 2024 would be any better, but for what it was worth, it felt good to finally turn the page and see how the new year would blossom from the seeds I had planted socially and professionally at the end of 2023.

Filled with hope and excitement, I returned to L.A. the day before New Year's Eve. Slowly but surely, my new life was beginning to take shape: structured and stable. My plan, as I envisioned it in my head, was to teach English during the week and go-go dance on the weekend. In between would be a mix of trivia nights, karaoke, hikes, volunteering, and other social activities I had only begun to explore. I was so excited and couldn't wait to get back to L.A.

I was told to arrive around eight o'clock for "painting", whatever that meant. I didn't question it, I was just beyond thrilled to have been offered a chance to make some money doing something I loved: being on stage.

After I arrived at the Sanctuary, I headed straight to the dressing room. It was more crowded than usual; it reminded me of a crowded submarine, but with a bunch of hot guys in nothing but their underwear. I checked in with Jaden, who was as professional and pleasant as he had been in December.

"Hey Jaden, Happy New Year!" I said as I extended my arms out for a hug.

"Hey, handsome! So excited to have you here, welcome," Jaden said. "Here is your uniform tonight."

A very tiny pair of black bikini cut briefs dangled from Jaden's left pinky. I took them and examined them front to back; they were very soft but very light material. Thankfully, they weren't white because I wasn't sure how that color would fare after getting hot and sweaty for four hours. I immediately ripped the tag in the back off and set my bag down, ready to undress.

"After you're in uniform, you're going to want to head out to the alley and get in line for painting. When you're done, just hang out and be ready to go on at nine," he instructed. "Here are the positions on this little spreadsheet right here. If you need help with the abbreviations, just ask one of the other dancers and they'll show you. You'll be on for half an hour, and then you'll break for half an hour until one in the morning. Sound good?"

"Sounds great, thanks!" I said.

Jaden winked at me and then headed out to another part of the bar. This was it, time to get dressed. Or, rather, undressed.

*Pinch me!*

I started with my sweatshirt and then my t-shirt, folding them neatly into my gym bag. Then, I stripped down to nothing, placed my cock ring on tightly around the goods, and slid on the tight black briefs. The bulkiness of my sweatshirt made it difficult to fit my black jeans into my bag, so I placed them on top of my bag in the corner of the room so they wouldn't get lost.

A few other dancers and I headed to the back alley behind the bar, where we would be individually painted by airbrush. As it turns out, on busy nights like New Year's Eve, big brands pay a lot of money to paint their logos on the go-go dancers. This night was a high-end vodka brand; each of us would have a mixture of rainbow colors and the vodka logo traced on various parts of our bodies.

*Jesus, I feel like I'm a branded car driving around the Indy 500. Shut up, be happy, slut.*

The weight of the evening was beginning to set in, and I was going through the process of getting done up for a big event. It felt exhilarating being "backstage" where all the behind-the-scenes action happened. I made my way outside and met up with the other dancers. Imposter syndrome popped out of nowhere. Some of the guys were a lot more muscular than I was, and even though I was toned, other guys were more toned than I was. I smacked myself, mentally.

*You are here for a reason. You were invited to dance here. You earned your spot here.*

As I waited in line, I began to scan the other boys and a few women who were in line. Cautious to not put my frigid bitch foot in my mouth again, I introduced myself to a few of the dancers immediately next to me in line. There were two guys and two girls. The lady dancers were both trained dancers, one from Maryland and the other from Australia. Not even two minutes into the conversation, it was clear that both of them had been training to be dancers since just after they could walk. I had immediate flashbacks to my horrendous dancing showcase days.

*You're going to look ridiculous on stage next to them. Whatever, I earned my spot here, and you, random voice in my head, are trapped up there and have no way of getting out. Bye-bye.*

The boys, Sal and Jason, were also very friendly when they introduced themselves. The conversation flowed so naturally; both of them were down-to-earth, very funny, and, more importantly, thought that I was very funny. Once the conversation took off, I felt much more in my element. Feelings of impostor syndrome waned, and I felt very comfortable being around the other dancers as well.

After a while, I began to wonder if this was all too good to be true; I was getting ready to be painted with a line of very attractive people, and not only were said attractive people sexy beyond all reason, but they were all, dare I say it, nice? Down to earth? Salt of the earth? Capable of carrying on a decent conversation?

*Keep your weapon at the ready, Beaver Cleaver. They're acting nice now but they might be bitches. Give them the benefit of the doubt and be pleasant, but don't be naïve.*

We continued the conversation a bit longer. The girls got painted and headed back inside. Sal and Jason introduced me to a few other dancers in line. Despite what we were about to do for work, we did not talk very much about sex or our bodies. The topics of conversation ranged from our upbringings, day jobs, and various interests and hobbies. I was struck by how introverted a lot of the dancers were based on their hobbies; a lot of comic book collectors, video gamers, and bookworms.

*It's perfectly acceptable to be both nerdy and sexy.*

After having the numbers of the new year and the vodka brand spray-painted onto me, I retreated backstage to the spreadsheet on the tablet. I may as well have been looking at a tablet with hieroglyphics on it. There were tons of names in the rows and abbreviations for each of the platforms in the columns. I had absolutely no idea which one was which. Since there were only a couple of spots left on the sheet, I just put my name in the first blank space I could find. Then I looked at the abbreviations for each of the four positions where I would be dancing. I looked around the dressing room to see if anyone could translate the spreadsheet hieroglyphics into plain English and then show me where the positions were in the club.

"Papi!" someone screamed from outside the dressing room.

"Who the—hey! Carlos! Feliz Nuevo Año!" I said.

We hugged and kissed multiple times on both cheeks.

"I told you that you'd make it! I'm so happy for you, mi amor," he said.

"I know you did! I'm so happy to see you! Hey, I need help deciphering the Rosetta Stone over here," I said sheepishly. "Where do I go for each of these sets?"

"Ok, let's see. Okay, so you're going to be on pole two, which is over on the side of the bar where they do the musicals night. There are five poles over there, and they are numbered from left to right. So, you would be on the second pole from the left. And it looks here like your third shift will be over on pole four, so same area," he explained.

He described the rest of the positions as clearly as he could, and yet I felt like how people usually feel when someone explains the rules to a new board game: every brain cell seemed to shut off.

"Ok, I may have to ask for a refresh just in case before I do each set, but I really appreciate the help, sexy boy," I said.

"Of course! Mi placer, it's going to be a fun night, baby. Just don't expect to make many tips tonight," Carlos said.

*Record scratch, I'm sorry, what?*

"I'm sorry, what? No tips on New Year's?" I asked.

"Yeah, because everything is just so expensive tonight, the drinks, the ride shares, the hotels, and there are more dancers here than usual, people aren't as generous with their tips," he explained. "And it's not like we're a karaoke machine and stop if nobody pays us. They get to see us for free. I know, bitches."

*Shit.*

"Well, I'll keep dancing like my life depends on it," I chuckled.

*I'm not even kidding. This was supposed to be how I was going to pay for food! Hope I make enough tips for a half a box of cornflakes.*

"You're going to do great, Papa," Carlos said as he gave me a big hug to which I responded by pinching his left butt cheek. "Aye, sexy papi, save that for later, diablito!"

As Carlos made his way out of the dressing room, some of the boys I had been chatting with outside came into the dressing room very excited. It was almost showtime.

I missed the very special bonding feeling that comes with performing with a group. The excitement that comes with preparing to appear on stage is one of the best feelings in the world. To commemorate the end of a year and an exciting night, one of the boys in the dressing room whipped out his phone to take a group selfie. We all huddled together and snapped a photo of all of us painted and scantily clad.

It was time to perform. The other dancers and I made our way out to our respective positions on the various stages, boxes, and poles around the club. We passed by patrons donning New Year's regalia and wielding more noisemakers than I cared to hear. Everyone had a glass full of booze and a heightened energy that would last the entire night.

I ascended onto pole number two for my first set. Almost instinctively, I went right into being in performance mode. Unlike my audition, I spent a minimal amount of time on the pole itself.

*Not today, Satan.*

Since my only experiences with go-go dancing before this were technically auditions, I felt much freer to explore dancing without the fear of messing up. I turned on the charm and started winking at people in the crowd, thrusting the goods on either side of the pole. The excitement of the evening began to explode exponentially, and I went into beast mode. I danced my heart out and began to break a sweat. My hands caressed my body, making their way up to the top of my head as I thrusted my glutes in either direction. A girl I went to high school with taught me that the way to shake your rear end is to not focus on the glute muscles, but rather squat down slightly and focus all the movement in your knees. This method was confirmed by both Javier and Carlos.

I danced a little too intensely during my first two sets, so by the halfway point, my body was exhausted and drenched in sweat. My third shift coincided with the Times Square ball drop that was streamed to coincide with California time. Jaden went around and called all the dancers to gather on the mainstage for the countdown.

We all gathered on top of the pair of L-shaped platforms where the audition was held. Amidst the excitement that permeated the room for the final three minutes of the year, I suddenly began to feel the same level of loneliness that I had felt when I was languishing back in Visalia. Friends had their arms around each other, and couples had their significant others to kiss. Even though I was on stage with other dancers, I was beginning to feel alone again. It didn't matter that I was surrounded by happy people; something inside me felt empty again.

*Oh, great. They're playing Dancing on My Own—another cliché.*

I closed my eyes, and my mind randomly flashed back to Gavin's Halloween party back in 2022.

Nearing the end of my volunteer gig with the campaign, I had yet to begin my depressive spiral. Gavin and Damien were hosting a party at Gavin's home. It was a standard gay Halloween party: lots of sexy costumes, flirty banter, and themed drinks to go around. After most of the partygoers had gone home, the handful of us who remained gathered in Gavin's big living room. He and I rummaged through his selection of records to keep the vibe going.

"I want to do Whitney! Play Whitney!" I insisted.

"We did Whitney last time you were here, let's get some variety," Gavin said.

"How about a musical?" I suggested. "We have almost enough people to be the von Trapp family singers. And, screw you, I get to be Maria this time."

"Damien will leave if we play another musical. I think he's been over-Hammersteined," Gavin said.

"Ok, just surprise us then," I said, making my way over to the couch and plopping myself into Damien's lap.

"Hello. And what would *you* like for Christmas?" Damien joked.

"Let's see. A win for our candidate next week, a lucrative job in D.C. or New York after we win, and a partridge in a pear tree," I said.

The remaining few guests piled onto the couch and began singing along to the music. Gavin had selected a "Divas of the '70s" record. We chatted about the party and life as we heard some of the greatest hits from Gloria Gaynor, Barbra Streisand, ABBA, Aretha Franklin, and Tina Turner. Then, the final song began to play. Appropriately, it was "Last Dance" by Donna Summer.

The intro of the song is very slow. A couple of us on the couch began lip syncing the words and singing dramatically into our fists like we were holding a microphone. As the song picked up the pace, I grabbed Damien and Gavin's wrists, and the rest of the couch followed suit, and we began dancing euphorically around.

We were dancing purely in the moment. I was not thinking about jobs, or my body, or the gym, or applications, or anything else. I felt neither the pre-election optimism nor the post-election pessimism. I felt no anxiety, depression, fear, anger, distress, loathing, or pain. All I felt was pure, unfiltered euphoria. It did not even feel like I was dancing, I was floating above time and space with people I cared most about. The only thing that mattered in that moment was love. I had forgotten that feeling, or at least buried it away after I began to spiral. Somehow, 14 months later, even though I was dancing on the stage of the most popular nightclub in all of West Hollywood to a packed audience, all I could think about was that night, dancing the last dance I would ever dance with Damien. I don't know if heaven exists, but if it does, I imagine that it would feel something like that Halloween night in Gavin's living room: absolute perfection.

"Ok, sexy bitches, we've got almost a minute left until midnight! Grab your honey, grab your drink, maybe grab both if you've got them. And let's ring this bitch in!" Carlos yelled into the microphone.

I opened my eyes again on the dance floor and felt a sense of peace, almost like I was still dancing back at Gavin's house. Suddenly, I did not feel lonely anymore. The music began to crescendo even louder, I could feel the sound waves reverberating throughout my body hair. I didn't know how many seconds were left in the countdown, but I didn't care. For the first time in over a year, I was fully present in the moment, finally able to embrace where I was in life and appreciate those around me.

Right as the clock started ticking down from ten, I stared into the crowd. Amidst a massive crowd shouting the countdown, I saw Terry standing there alone, staring directly at me. He had that same look Enrique had when I danced in Denver, and Damien had when I danced in Fresno. I wondered how many people over the last year and a half had given me that look when I wasn't looking.

This time, I was not going to take that look for granted. So I danced for Enrique, who couldn't be there in person, and Damien, who could only be there in spirit, and Terry, who stood before me in the flesh. I danced for the countless people who supported me when I needed it most and saw me at my best, even at my worst.

Five seconds left in 2023. The music was now blasting at full volume, the lights flashed blindingly around the club like a supernova, and the crowd continued shouting the numbers as they quickly approached zero. Three, two...one. I winked at Terry, and he smiled back. Happy New Year.

# Epilogue

Happy ending, right? Well, as of this writing, I'm still alive, so life is still moving; the roller coaster has not stopped.

After an uncharacteristically rainy winter in Southern California, in the following months after New Year's, the foot traffic at the bars slowed to a snail's pace. Bookings from Sanctuary, Charlie, and other promoters with whom Carlos had put me in contact decreased in tandem. This is typical of nightlife: some weekends are packed to the brim with gigs, others not so much. Our bookings are completely tethered to the basic fundamentals of supply and demand: we're in business when the bars are busy but when they aren't, we're screwed. Regardless, as a performer, I will always go wherever I'm booked and put in 150%. Always.

By the end of May that year, after feeling deeply distressed about my financial situation and seeing the shine of a new city wear off, I started to fall into the same bad habits that precipitated my downward spiral the previous year. However, with the hindsight of history and a better understanding of myself, thanks to therapy, I made a conscious choice to snap out of it. Instead of stewing in my negative, intrusive thoughts alone or with alcohol, I volunteered more, spent more time out at trivia and karaoke nights, and vented to my friends in person.

During one particular weekend that month, a new friend of mine encouraged me to just enjoy myself and not dwell on bookings, promoters, or anything other than having fun. As I've mentioned earlier, I really hate it when my friends are right. I'm glad I kept my chin up because the one gig I had that weekend yielded me a wonderful surprise.

In between my shifts at the bar that night, I ran into the kitchen on my way to the dressing room. This particular bar sold pizzas, so the kitchen was lined with several very hot, steamy ovens. As soon as I pushed through the swinging doors, I saw none other than Kesha surrounded by her team. Having just performed onstage in WeHo, she was drenched in sweat from head to toe.

*Me too, girl.*

Taken aback, I made every possible effort to maintain a straight face as I walked into the kitchen. The little group huddled around Kesha was fanning her with their bare hands; one of them was pointing one of those little fans you buy at a theme park at her face. On my way passing them, I stopped myself in front of the group.

"You know there's a walk-in refrigerator right behind you, right?" I asked.

Kesha and her crew stared ahead at me, blankly. Then they looked over at the refrigerator door before turning their heads back at me like I had discovered gold.

"Oh my god! You're our hero!" her assistant yelled as the other members of her group began applauding.

After yanking the titanium handle and opening the fridge, I walked in first to the walk-in fridge that sat around 40 degrees Fahrenheit. Kesha followed right behind me, and her crew filed in after.

*Um, so. You're nose to nose. With Kesha. 95% naked. In a refrigerator. Holy shit. Another late participant for my bingo card.*

"Hey, thanks, doll," Kesha said, touching my shoulder.

*What. The. Fuck.*

"No problem! This is a great place to shack up if you need a little breeze," I said.

"You're the best! You know this is Kesha, right?" her assistant asked.

*Act dumb! Play it cool!*

"Oh, I thought I recognized you!" I said back with a wink.

After her crew passed us waters, Kesha and I chatted briefly. She was perfectly lovely and thanked me for bringing her to the chilled room so we could all cool down.

*There's a sentence I never thought I would ever say.*

"Can we all do a shot together?" her assistant asked.

*And another sentence I never thought I'd hear.*

"Are you down, babe?" Kesha asked me.

*Ok, I'm just going to stop acting shocked. Let's do it.*

"Down," I said.

After we had tubes of shots in our hands, we toasted, clinked our tubes together, and it was bottoms up. Cautious of the time, I made sure to grab a quick photo before I left. Kesha and I both snapped a selfie on our phones before sharing a sweaty side hug and then parting ways. I don't think I will ever ring in the month of June in a more spontaneous and special way.

After being grumpy and pessimistic for a week, another friend had yet again pushed me to be a better version of myself when all I wanted to just sulk and be alone. I was still susceptible to the temptations of old habits, and still am, but now have a more solid foundation and the benefit of hindsight to guide me. I've learned that I'm at my best when I'm around people who not only lift me up but also challenge me. I'm at my worst when I'm alone, marinating myself in the worst idealized versions of myself.

In the weeks and months following, I continued to find ways to keep myself away from a lonely bedroom. Later in the fall, I joined the Gay Men's Chorus of Los Angeles and was introduced to the most fabulous group of singers that I continue to regard as chosen family. Having the ability to make music with a talented group has been an absolute breath of fresh air. Since I've joined, a lot of the men in the chorus have shared with me their own experiences with depression, social isolation, despair, and self-medication. It only confirmed the mantras I had learned in therapy about being in darkness alone and dancing in the flames.

Institutions that used to be the bedrock of order and stability in our society are crumbling quickly, which has led to many people, particularly young men, slipping through the cracks and resorting to acts of aggression and even violence. Had I not had the type of upbringing and positive community surrounding me during my dark period, I'm sure some of the situations I've described in this book would have ended differently, and certainly not for the better. I'm one of the lucky ones.

If men were truly more open to asking for help and being honest and vulnerable about how we feel, I think we wouldn't succumb so easily to these bad habits. After all, alcohol and lying in bed all day are both cheaper than therapy, so that will always be the go-to unless there is a change.

The only antidote to misery is more community: people that treat you like an individual deserving of love, people that check in on you at random hours of the day, people that drive more than a few minutes to see you just to see you, or people that are with you when you are at your worst but see you like you're at your best.

I'm still young, I still have a life ahead of me, the roller coaster is going to keep moving, whether I like it or not. I'm glad I experienced heartache and despair because it has ensured that I won't take for granted the wonderful people who have been and will always be by my side, whether I'm on the kitchen floor or the dance floor. I hope that you have people, even if it's just one person, with whom you can enjoy a dance in the flames. It's the greatest feeling in the world. Trust me.

# Acknowledgments

The publication of this book would not have been possible without, well, a village.

To my family: thank you for your patience, love, and understanding as I worked through not only the process of writing this memoir but also the many events that shaped it.

To my friends: those who have stood by me, either physically or metaphorically, when I needed love the most. Your presence saved me more times than you know.

To the drag queens: thank you for never being short of positivity, vitality, encouragement, and joy. It's an honor to be in the trenches together.

To all therapists, mentors, and community groups: you are angels among us.

To those struggling with mental health, addiction, or loneliness: help is always there; all you have to do is ask for it. Please read the following pages for resources.

To the readers: thank you for hopping on the roller coaster, hope you didn't puke.

And to the friend who referred my phone number to the hotline, thank you.

# Resources

Crisis Support

988 Suicide & Crisis Lifeline (US) – Call or text 988

Available 24/7 for free and confidential support.

Website: https://988lifeline.org

SAMHSA National Helpline – 1-800-662-HELP (4357)

Free, confidential help for substance use and mental health issues.

Website: https://www.samhsa.gov/find-help/national-helpline

Therapy and Mental Health Support

Better Help – https://www.betterhelp.com

Online therapy with licensed professionals. Options for financial aid.

Open Path Collective – https://www.openpathcollective.org

Affordable therapy (sessions starting at $30–$60).

Man Therapy – https://mantherapy.org

A humorous, yet sincere site focused on men's mental health with tools and resources.

Alcohol Use and Sobriety

Alcoholics Anonymous (AA) – https://www.aa.org

Global peer support network for those seeking sobriety.

SMART Recovery – https://www.smartrecovery.org

Science-based alternative to AA that focuses on cognitive behavioral tools.

The Tempest Sobriety School (for men) – https://jointempest.com (Note: Mostly online sobriety support, may focus more on the general population, but often includes male-specific resources.)

### Men's Groups and Community

Movember – https://us.movember.com

Supports mental health, suicide prevention, and prostate/testicular cancer. Offers content and initiatives for men's well-being.

Heads Up Guys – https://headsupguys.org

Specific to men's depression and suicide prevention, it includes self-checks and recovery plans.

The Mankind Project – https://mankindproject.org

Personal development and support groups for men seeking emotional maturity and growth.

Evryman – https://evryman.com

Men's groups and retreats to foster connection and emotional resilience.